303
TRICKY
CHESS
TACTICS

ACKNOWLEDGEMENTS

A special thanks to the beautiful and mysterious Riley Kellogg who checked, corrected, proofed, and solved. But mostly it was Riley who spun her magic and made the computer hum to her tune. Others who contributed positions, checked solutions, or made useful suggestions include: Adam Marcus, Tom Schrade, Jeff Ivins, Mike Senkiewicz, Emmit Jefferson, Michele Lance, Jeff Tannenbaum, Sari Glickstein, Steve Anderson, Ben Schanback, Jeremy Gross, Julian Katz-Samuels, Dan Satterwaite, Michael Puopolo, Alex Jarrell, Glen Hart, Andy Fox, Andy Ansell, Oshon Temple, Peter Winik, Nathan Resika, Alex Rasic, Ned Wall, and Peter J. Tamburro, Jr.

ABOUT THE AUTHORS

FRED WILSON

Fred Wilson is among the finest chess teachers and authors. Wilson has authored *303 Tricky Chess Tactics*, *303 Tricky Chess Puzzles*, *303 More Tricky Chess Puzzles*, and *303 Tricky Checkmates* with Bruce Alberston for Cardoza Publishing. He is the owner of Fred Wilson Chess Books in New York City.

BRUCE ALBERSTON

Bruce Alberston, a well-known chess trainer and teacher in the New York city area, collaborated with Fred Wilson on *202 Surprising Mates*, *303 Tricky Chess Tactics*, *303 Tricky Chess Puzzles*, *303 More Tricky Chess Puzzles*, and *303 Tricky Checkmates* with Wilson. He is also the sole author of two books: *51 Chess Openings* and *Chess Opening Trap of the Day*. Alberston did significant research and analysis for Bruce Pandolfini (who has written 17 books for Simon & Shuster).

FRED WILSON & BRUCE ALBERSTON

303 TRICKY CHESS TACTICS

CARDOZA PUBLISHING

Cardoza Publishing is the foremost gaming publisher in the world, with a library of over 200 up-to-date and easy-to-read books and strategies. These authoritative works are written by the top experts in their fields and with more than 10,000,000 books in print, represent the best-selling and most popular gaming books anywhere.

2018 EDITION

Library of Congress Catalog Card No: 2017955731
ISBN: 978-1-58042-348-9

Visit our web site—www.cardozabooks.com—or write
for a full list of books and computer strategies.

CARDOZA PUBLISHING
P.O. Box 98115, Las Vegas, NV 89193
Phone (800) 577-WINS
email: cardozabooks@aol.com

TABLE OF CONTENTS

SYMBOLS AND ABBREVIATIONS

K stands for King
Q stands for Queen
R stands for Rook
B stands for Bishop
N stands for Knight
There is no symbol for the pawn. A pawn move is indicated by a lowercase letter which identifies the file of the moving pawn. (e4 shows that a pawn has moved to the e4 square. If a capital letter had preceded the letter, such as Ne4, it would shows a piece had moved there, in this case, the Knight.)

---

x stands for a capture
0-0 stands for King-side castling
0-0-0 stands for Queen-side castling

... the three dots following a move number indicate a Black move. (2...e6 indicates that Black's second move was to bring the pawn to e6.)
/ with a capital letter immediately to the right of the slash mark indicates that a pawn is promoted to a piece. (h1/Q shows that the pawn on the h file moved to the h1 square – thus a Black pawn – and was promoted to a Queen.)

+ stands for check
# stands for checkmate

! means very good move
!! means brilliant move
? means bad move
?? means losing blunder

INTRODUCTION

Chess is 99% tactics — Richard Teichmann

Strategy is a case of thinking, tactics one of seeing — Max Euwe

Chess is an unforgiving game — Emmitt Jefferson.

Do you really know what tactics are? Or, why they are so important? And why, whenever tactics are discussed, they are almost always linked with the term strategy? As chess teachers with many years experience, we are constantly amazed and a bit dismayed to see how many beginning and intermediate chessplayers can neither accurately define nor fully appreciate the importance of strategy and tactics. So, let's begin with some definitions:

Strategy is your overall plan in any given position towards a specific goal. While it is often an aggressive plan, it can also be defensive, depending upon your analysis and understanding of the needs of the position.

Tactics are short-term maneuvers which always involve either threats, captures or combinations. Since the majority of good tactics are created with successful combinations, this term also requires a clear definition: A **combination** is a tactical maneuver in which you sacrifice material to obtain an advantage, or at least to improve your position. So strategy then, is your general plan, while tactics are your specific means of carrying it out.

7

At every level, from beginner through grandmaster, it is impossible to increase your overall strength without a corresponding increase in your tactical ability. You must practice solving positions with tactical solutions until you become comfortable with all the standard concepts.

In *303 Tricky Chess Tactics*, we have created a basic tactics workbook which you should go through as many times as necessary until you are able to recognize and solve all the standard tactical themes. We have organized the book into six chapters, reflecting, in our opinion, the frequency with which typical tactical opportunities occur. Hopefully, you will begin to develop a type of pattern recognition for sensing tactical possibilities in the many different kinds of positions. A full third of the book is devoted to forks (also often called double attacks) and pins, these clearly being the most commonly used tactics.

Perhaps the most dramatic illustration of successfully improving one's pattern recognition of a forking situation can be seen in the Moscow City Championship of 1956, when 26 year old Tigran Petrosian played **1.Nxf7** and Simagin forced a draw by perpetual check beginning with **1...Qd1+**. Hmm...

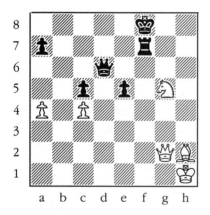

Petrosian-Simagin, Moscow, 1956

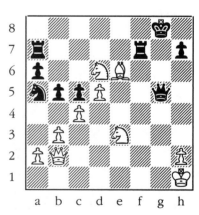

Petrosian-Spassky, Moscow, 1966

Do you see what Petrosian should have done? Well, Petrosian certainly learned his lesson, for 10 years later during his exciting World Championship Match with Spassky, the older and much wiser Petrosian finished off his rival with the following spectacular forking combination: **1.Bxf7+ Rxf7 2.Qh8+!! Kxh8 3.Nxf7+** winning back the Queen, emerging a Knight and a Pawn ahead.

So, now, with the benefit of hindsight (pattern recognition!), can you find what Petrosian missed against Simagin? (Answer: **1.Qa8+! Kg7 2.Bxe5+! Qxe5 3.Qh8+!! Kxh8 4.Nxf7+** and **5.Nxe5** with a won endgame.)

We recently had our belief in the value of practicing pattern recognition confirmed when showing the following two positions to a group of average adult players during a lecture. In both examples, it is Black to Move.

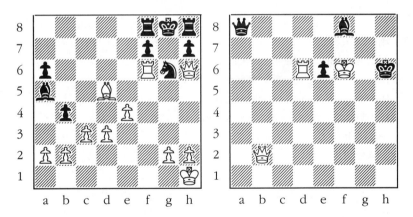

In the first position, above left, from the Tarrasch-Tchigorin Match in 1893, it took from thirty to sixty seconds for most of the players to figure out why Black (Tchigorin) resigned! One fellow even asked why Black didn't play **1...bxc3 2.bxc3(?) Bxc3.** He said "and now doesn't Black have some fighting chances with a Rook and Knight for his Queen?" Had he done more work solving tactical positions, the operative tactic here, namely the deadly pin on the f7 Pawn by the mighty Bishop on **d5**, should have screamed out at him. Indeed, we hope you noticed that Tchigorin resigned because Black has no saving move at all to counter the upcoming double capture on g6. (For example, **1...bxc3 2.Rxg6+! hxg6 3.Qxg6#**, a neat epaulette mate).

In the next position (above right), surprisingly it still took most of these decent players about 20-30 seconds to see that Black wins with the simple skewer **1...Bg7+**. Any experienced player would have immediately noticed White's King and Queen on the same diagonal and, especially in such a wide-open position, begin looking for skewering opportunities. Seeing the possibilities for such standard tactics as forks, pins, skewers, and discoveries, can be achieved quickly, but, unless you're a born chess genius like Capablanca or Fischer, not without practice… and a little work!

We have made this work easier for you by our arrangement of the material. Every chapter is prefaced by a clear and concise explanation of the mechanism that operates and distinguishes the tactics under discussion, followed by a carefully chosen selection of examples, gradually increasing in difficulty. Over a third of the positions used in this book are with Black to Move, as we feel it is important to consider situations from Black's perspective.

We have purposely used only two large, clear diagrams per page so as not to discourage you from really trying to visualize possible continuations.

While many of the tactics examined herein will be familiar to most of you, we feel that two of the less common ones, trapping and Pawn promotion, have been oddly neglected by the pedagogic literature. Consider the following two positions, Black to Move in each case:

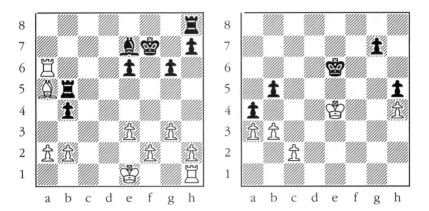

Often, no combination is necessary for trapping tactics to succeed. You are only required to see the vulnerability of a certain piece in a given position. How can Black win a piece in the first position above left? Answer: **1...Rc8** (threatening to win the h1 Rook with the skewer **2...Rc1+**) **2.0-0** (other King moves lead to the same result) **R8c5! 3.Bb6 Rc6** pinning and winning White's Bishop.

Notice how methodical Black's winning moves were; no sacrifices, nothing fancy. Also, be aware that you may sometimes use several different tactics in creating a winning sequence of moves. Here, Black first threatened a skewer, then established a pin before White succumbed to the overiding trapping idea.

In the second position on the previous page, White has just played **1.b3**, hoping to eventually win this endgame by establishing a passed Pawn on the Queenside. This is a blunder we have even seen grandmasters make! Why? Because after Black plays **1...b4!** he can force a Pawn through to Queen on the a-file whether White captures or not! Amateurs are particularly vulnerable to promotion tactics, which is odd because when you think about it, as the great chess teacher and author Fred Reinfeld pointed out, "if checkmating your opponent is the strongest move in chess... (then) Queening a Pawn successfully is the second strongest move!"

Finally, we have ended this book with a most unusual and little-understood tactic—how to force a draw in a difficult position. We hope you study these last seventeen examples carefully. They may save you some valuable half-points!

We will leave you with the observation that, with the exception of some mating attacks, most of the tactics in our book involve winning material, sometimes even only a single Pawn or just the exchange (for example, winning a Rook for a Bishop or a Knight). This is the nitty-gritty of chess. It is essentially a ma-terialistic game where superior force will usually win.

The witty and somewhat cynical grandmaster Saviely Tarta-kower once remarked that "tactics is what you do when there's something to do, strategy what you do when there's nothing to do." We hope that by working through our book carefully, you will soon discover many more opportunities in your own games for "something to do!"

Go get 'em.

Fred Wilson & Bruce Alberston

CHAPTER 1

THE FORK

THE FORK

The most common form of double attack is the **fork**, a simultaneous attack by one unit against two hostile units. The aggressor unit inserts itself at some midpoint, between the two attacked units, and the defender finds, to his chagrin, that he can save one of his men, but not both.

In theory, any chess piece has the capability of forking two enemy pieces. Knight forks and Queen forks occur with most frequency, then come Bishop, Rook, and pawn forks. A fork by the King is rarely seen and so we give no practical examples.

ORGANIZATION

The arrangement of positions is according to the piece that is doing the forking. Knight forks are the trickiest, so they get the most attention.

1–20	Knight Forks
21–31	Queen Forks
32–40	Bishop Forks
41–46	Rook Forks
47–50	Pawn Forks

REMINDER

Check out the caption above each position so you know whose turn it is to move: White or Black. Also note that within each sub-group, the problems increase in difficulty.

Black to Move

1.

White to Move

2.

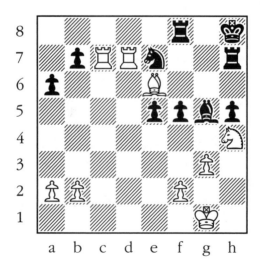

Black to Move

3.

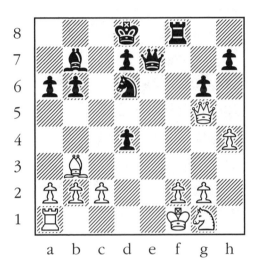

Black to Move

4.

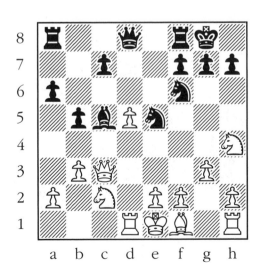

White to Move

5.

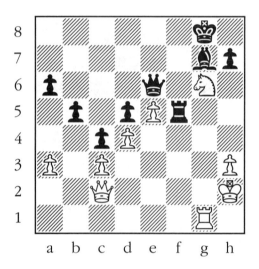

White to Move

6.

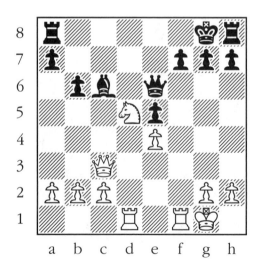

White to Move

7.

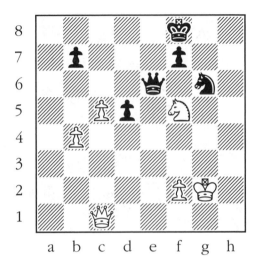

White to Move

8.

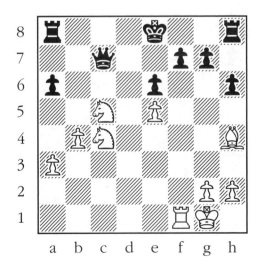

White to Move

9.

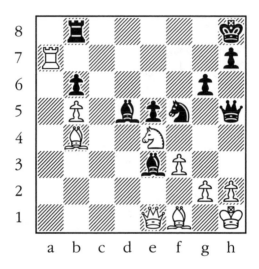

Black to Move

10.

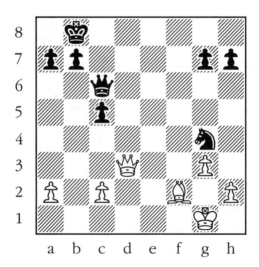

White to Move

11.

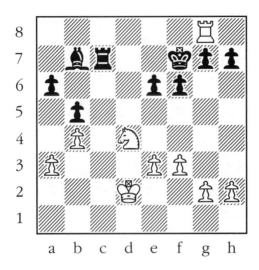

Black to Move

12.

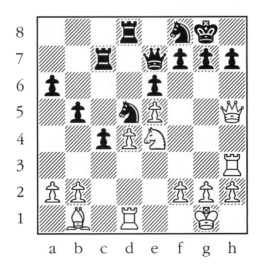

White to Move

13.

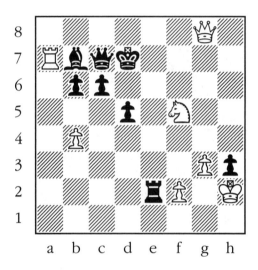

Black to Move

14.

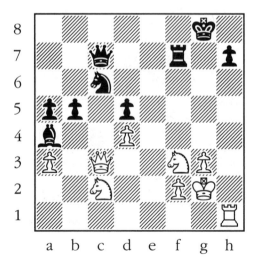

Black to Move

15.

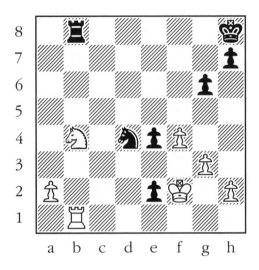

White to Move

16.

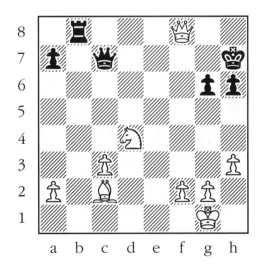

Black to Move

17.

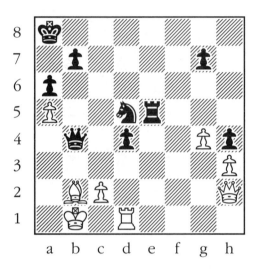

Black to Move

18.

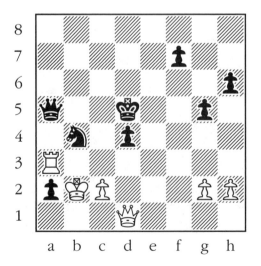

Black to Move

19.

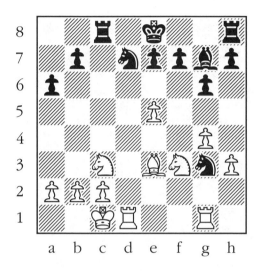

White to Move

20.

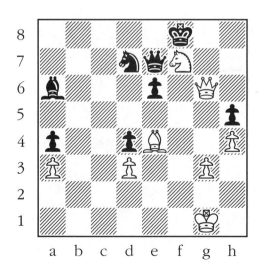

Black to Move

21.

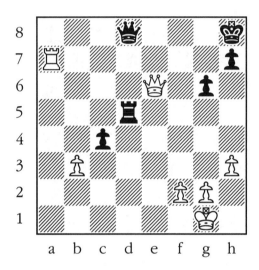

White to Move

22.

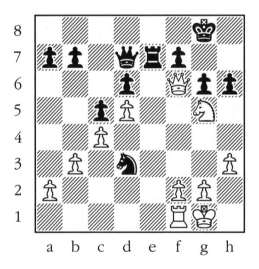

Black to Move

23.

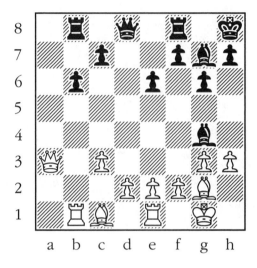

Black to Move

24.

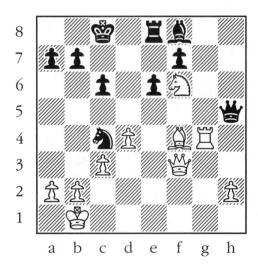

White to Move

25.

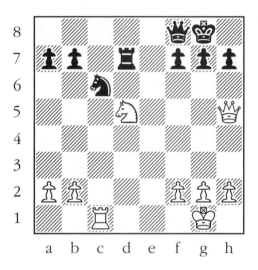

Black to Move

26.

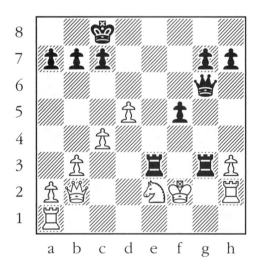

Black to Move

27.

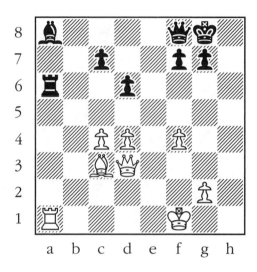

White to Move

28.

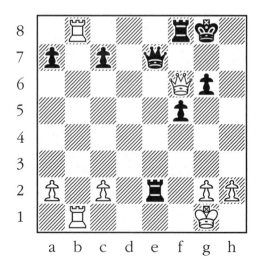

White to Move

29.

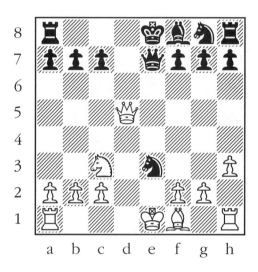

White to Move

30.

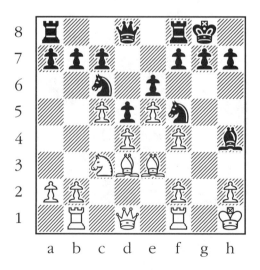

Black to Move

31.

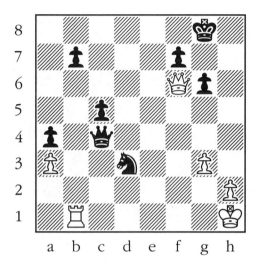

Black to Move

32.

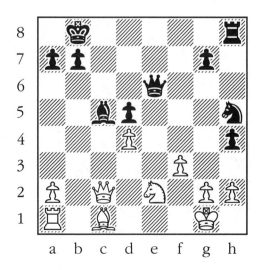

Black to Move

33.

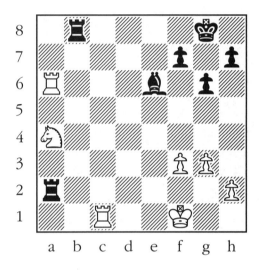

Black to Move

34.

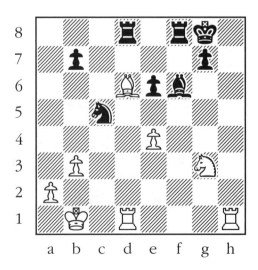

White to Move

35.

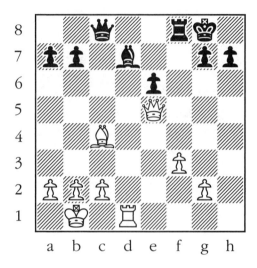

Black to Move

36.

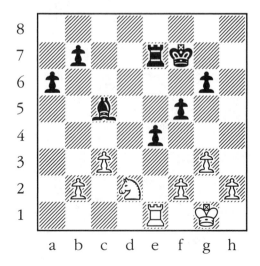

Black to Move

37.

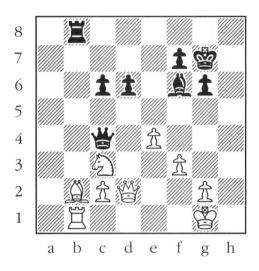

White to Move

38.

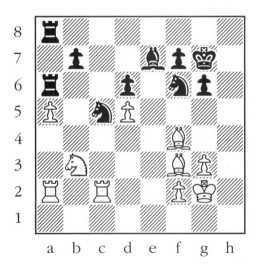

White to Move

39.

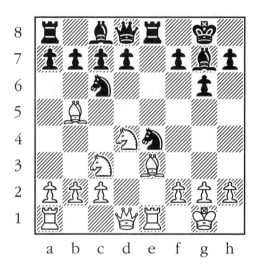

White to Move

40.

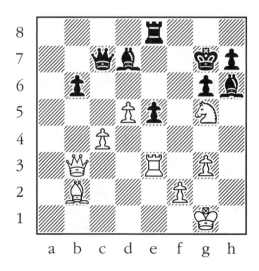

White to Move

41.

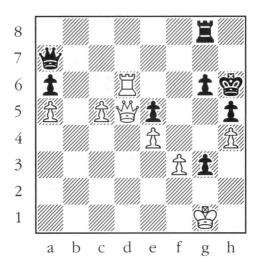

White to Move

42.

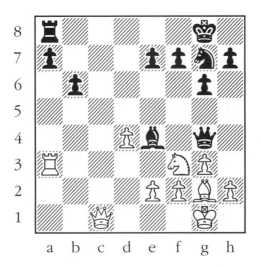

Black to Move

43.

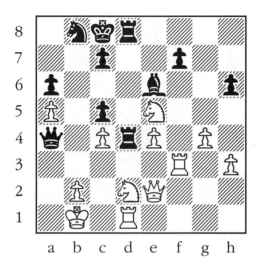

White to Move

44.

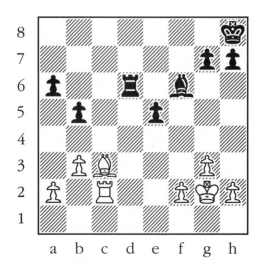

Black to Move

45.

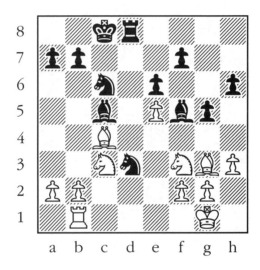

Black to Move

46.

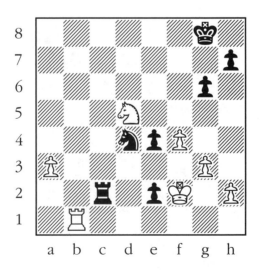

Black to Move

47.

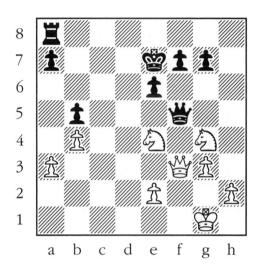

White to Move

48.

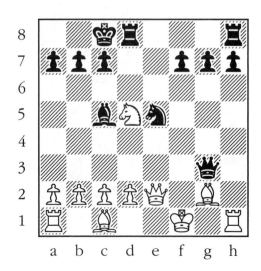

Black to Move

49.

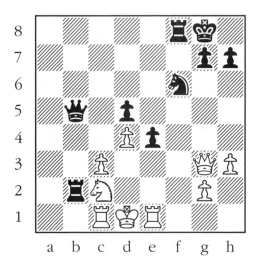

White to Move

50.

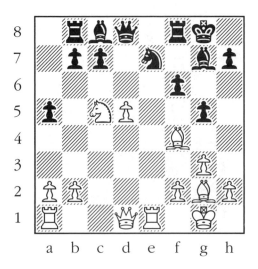

CHAPTER TWO

THE PIN

THE PIN

The **pin** is a tactic that can only be performed by a line piece: a Bishop, Rook, or Queen. The line piece directly attacks an enemy unit, the pinned piece, who in turn shields or screens a more valuable piece, standing to the rear. These are the three main actors in a pin: the pinning piece, the pinned piece, and the screened piece. Should the pinned piece move off the line, the screened piece then falls to a capture, not at all a desirable prospect for the defender.

Occasionally the screened objective is not a piece at all, but a critical square, an entry point. Again, if the pinned piece moves off the line, the attacking piece enters the critical square, usually with fatal effect to the King.

ORGANIZATION

The layout of this chapter is by the rearmost piece in the lineup, the screened piece. You'll start spotting pinning opportunities when you train your eye to see all the way down the attacking line, to the screened objective at the other end.

51–77	Screened King
78–86	Screened Queen
87–95	Screened Rook
96–100	Screened Entry Square

Black to Move

51.

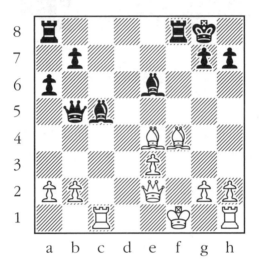

White to Move

52.

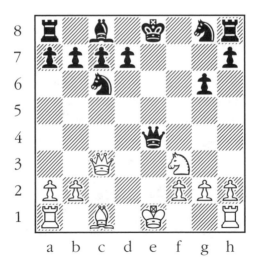

Black to Move

53.

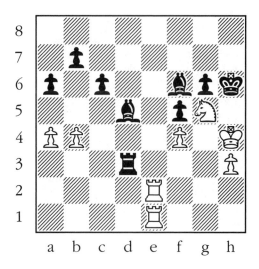

White to Move

54.

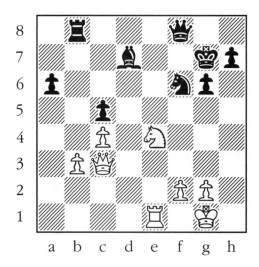

White to Move

55.

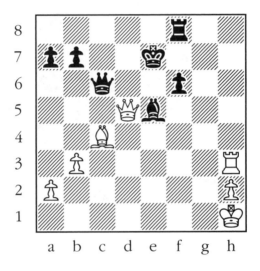

White to Move

56.

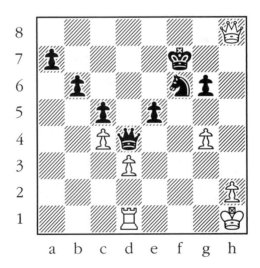

White to Move

57.

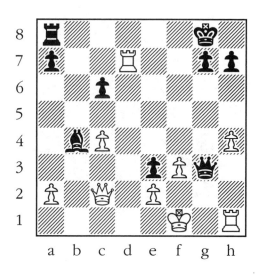

White to Move

58.

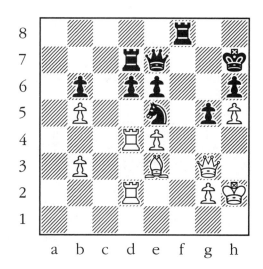

White to Move

59.

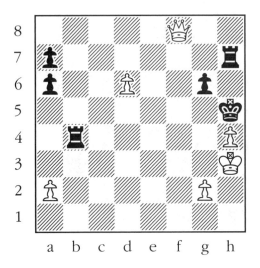

Black to Move

60.

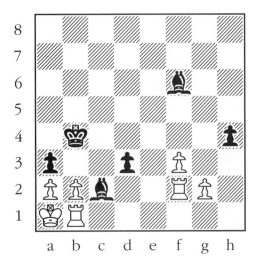

White to Move

61.

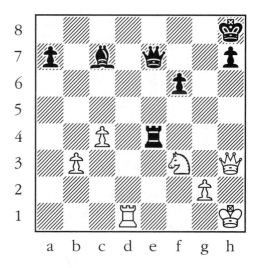

White to Move

62.

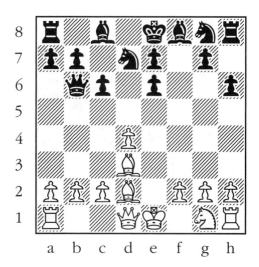

45

Black to Move

63.

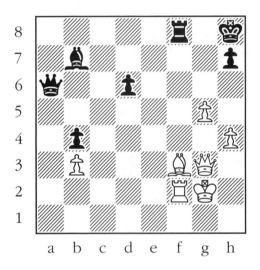

White to Move

64.

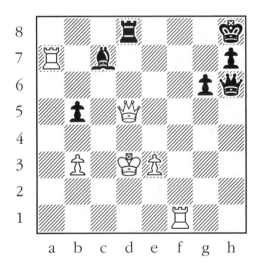

White to Move

65.

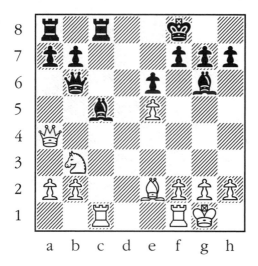

Black to Move

66.

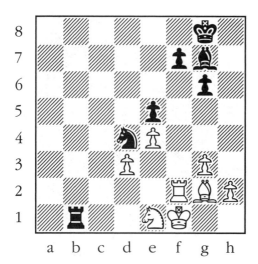

Black to Move

67.

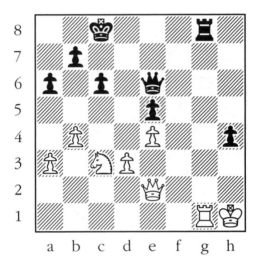

White to Move

68.

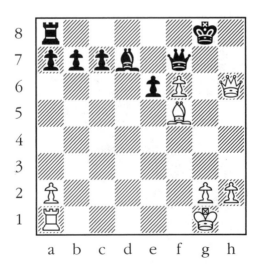

Black to Move

69.

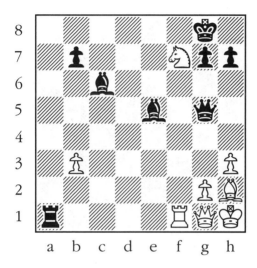

White to Move

70.

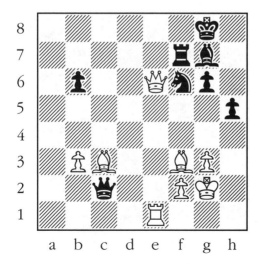

White to Move

71.

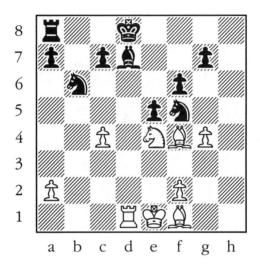

White to Move

72.

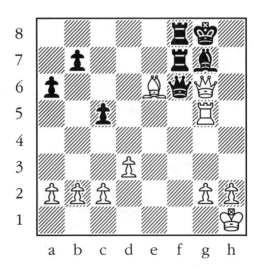

White to Move

73.

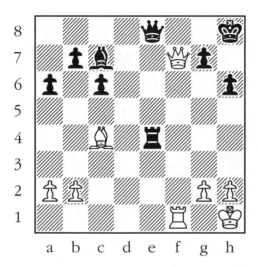

White to Move

74.

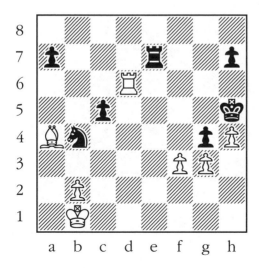

White to Move

75.

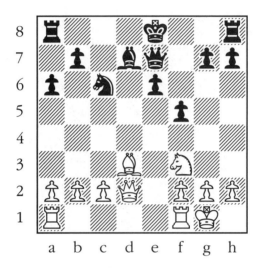

White to Move

76.

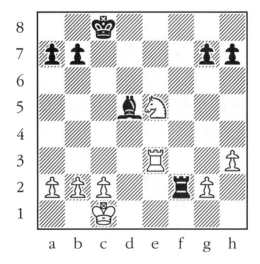

Black to Move

77.

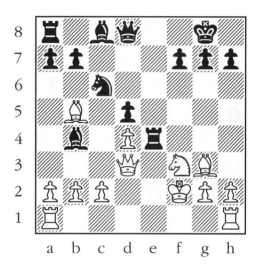

Black to Move

78.

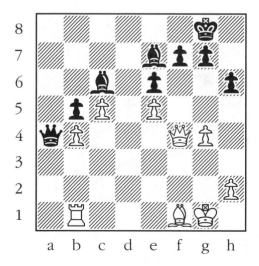

White to Move

79.

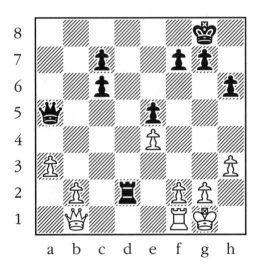

White to Move

80.

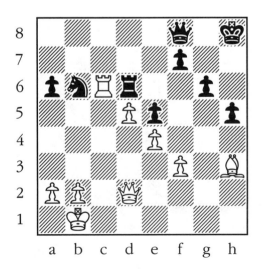

Black to Move

81.

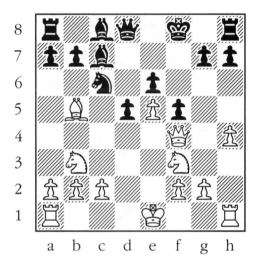

White to Move

82.

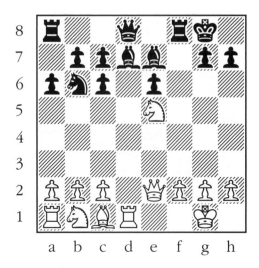

Black to Move

83.

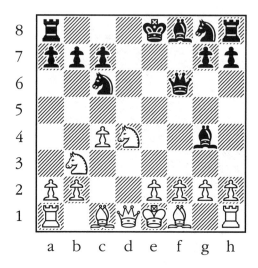

White to Move

84.

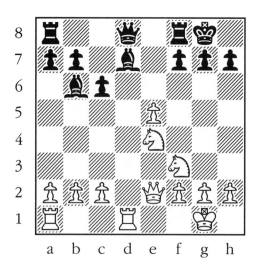

Black to Move

85.

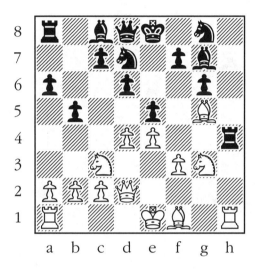

Black to Move

86.

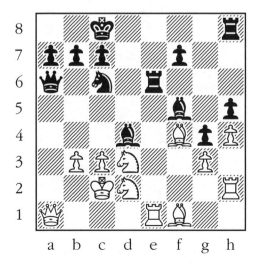

Black to Move

87.

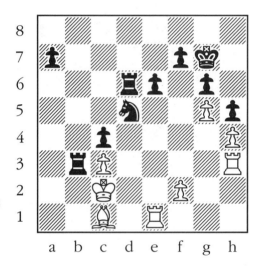

Black to Move

88.

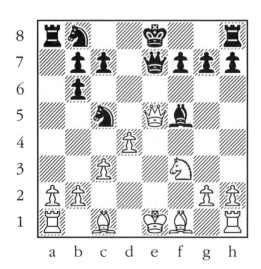

White to Move

89.

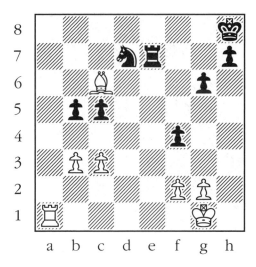

Black to Move

90.

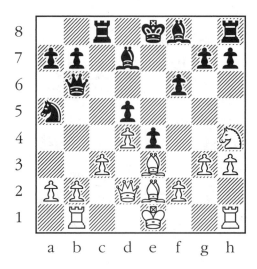

White to Move

91.

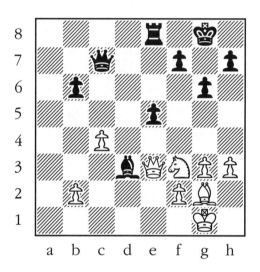

Black to Move

92.

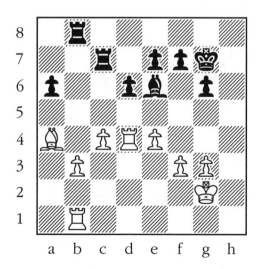

White to Move

93.

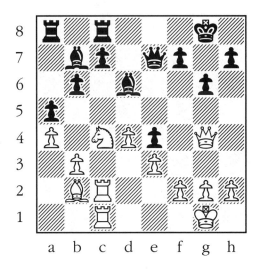

White to Move

94.

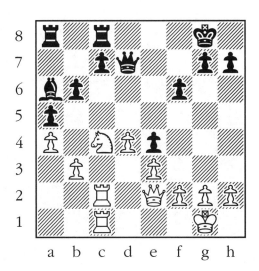

White to Move

95.

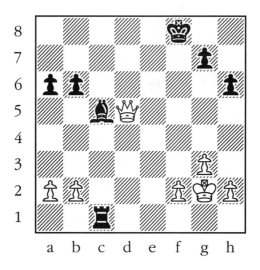

Black to Move

96.

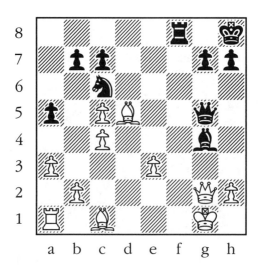

Black to Move

97.

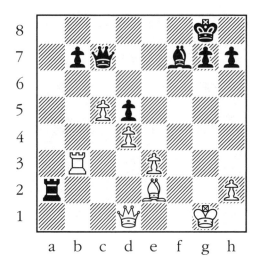

White to Move

98.

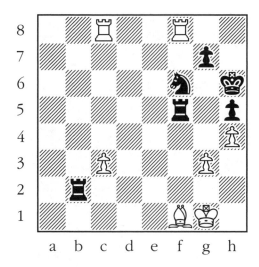

White to Move

99.

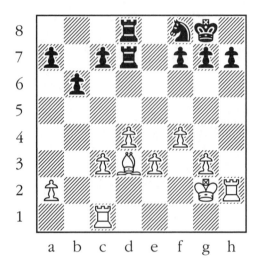

White to Move

100.

CHAPTER THREE

DISCOVERIES AND SKEWERS

DISCOVERIES AND SKEWERS

Both discoveries and skewers are tactical devices which require use of an open line. The **skewer**, a reverse cousin of the pin, is a three piece line up, with an attacking unit and two enemy units, all posted on the same open line. In the skewer, it is the more valuable of the two pieces which receives the brunt of the initial attack. When it moves down off the attacking line, the piece to the rear becomes subject to capture

The **discovery**, another three piece lineup, illustrates the idea of a masked attack. A piece moving off an open line, unmasks an attack by a piece stationed in the rear. The attack by the stationary piece has to be dealt with immediately; this is particularly true if it is a discovered check to the King. But meanwhile, the moving piece is free to roam and inflict maximum damage.

ORGANIZATION

Discoveries are arranged by the roving piece which accomplishes the unmasking. It is the middle piece in the lineup. The same arrangement, the middle piece in the lineup, is also used for skewers.

White to Move

101.

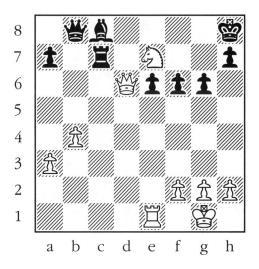

White to Move

102.

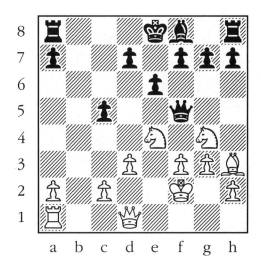

Black to Move

103.

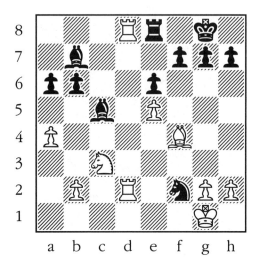

White to Move

104.

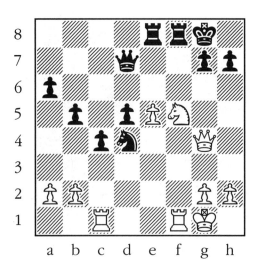

Black to Move

105.

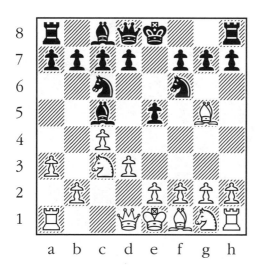

Black to Move

106.

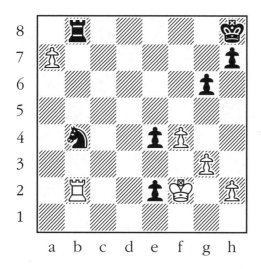

Black to Move

107.

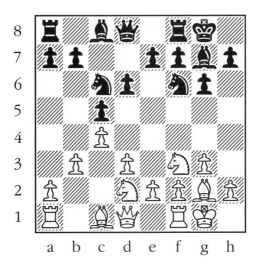

White to Move

108.

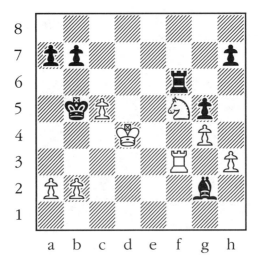

White to Move

109.

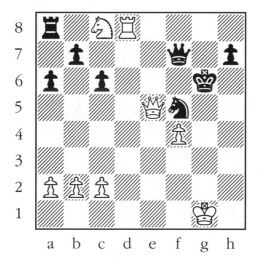

White to Move

110.

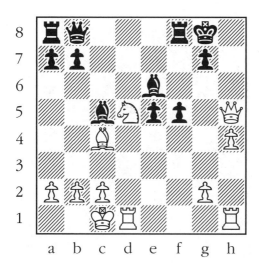

White to Move

111.

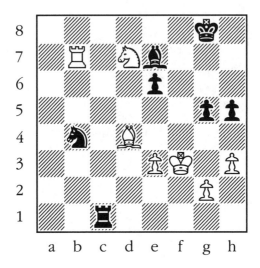

Black to Move

112.

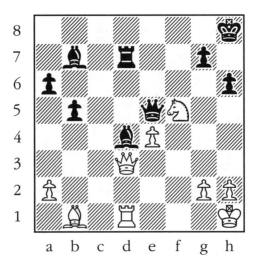

Black to Move

113.

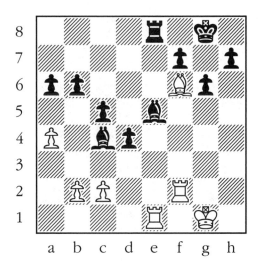

Black to Move

114.

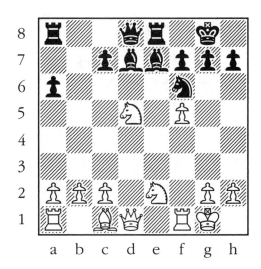

Black to Move

115.

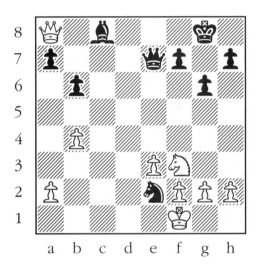

White to Move

116.

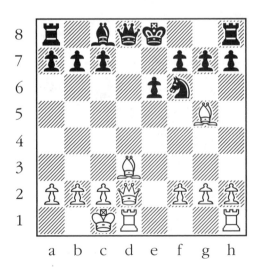

Black to Move

117.

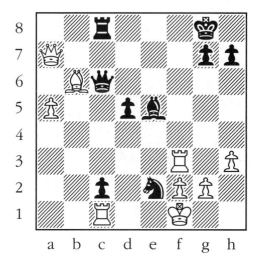

White to Move

118.

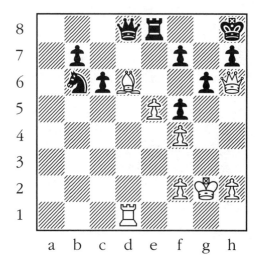

White to Move

119.

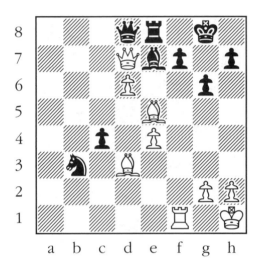

Black to Move

120.

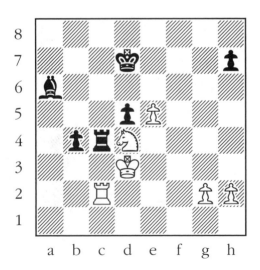

Black to Move

121.

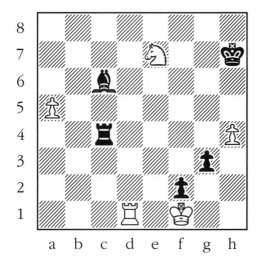

Black to Move

122.

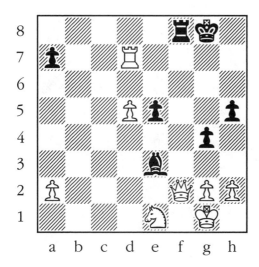

Black to Move

123.

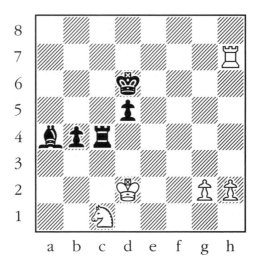

White to Move

124.

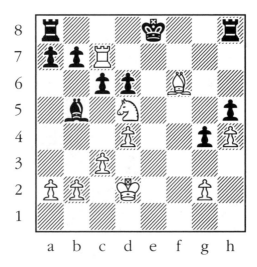

Black to Move

125.

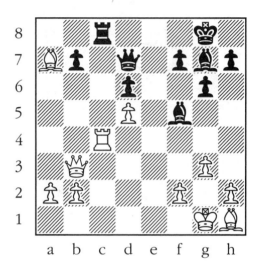

Black to Move

126.

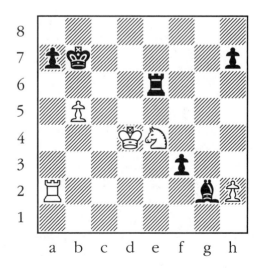

White to Move

127.

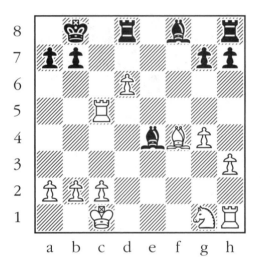

White to Move

128.

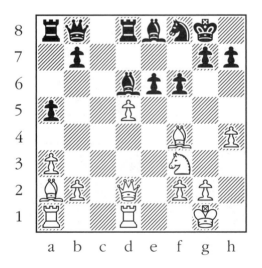

Black to Move

129.

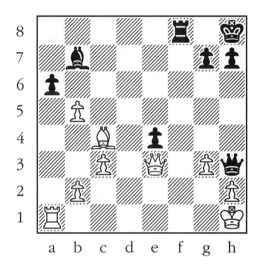

White to Move

130.

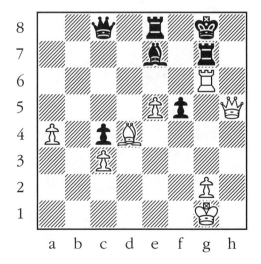

White to Move

131.

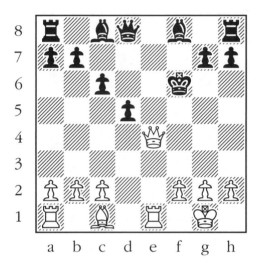

White to Move

132.

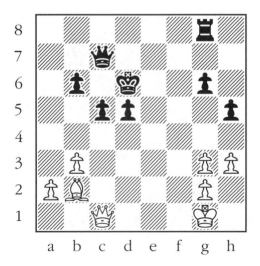

White to Move

133.

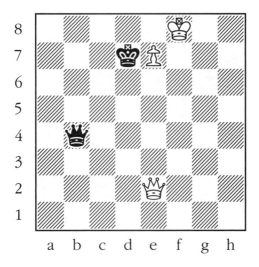

White to Move

134.

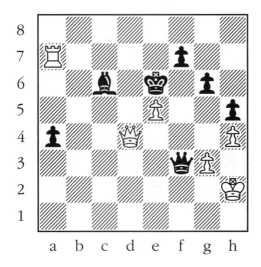

White to Move

135.

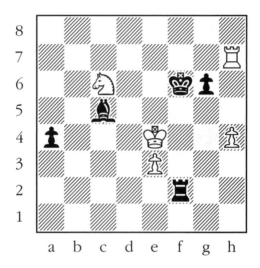

White to Move

136.

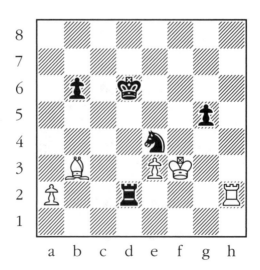

White to Move

137.

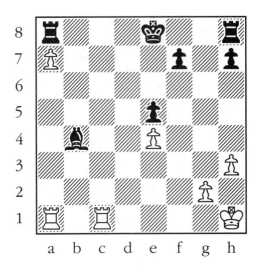

Black to Move

138.

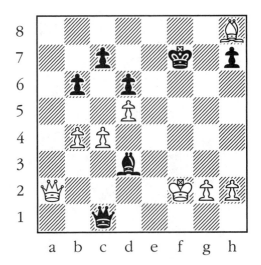

White to Move

139.

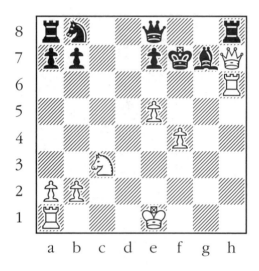

White to Move

140.

White to Move

141.

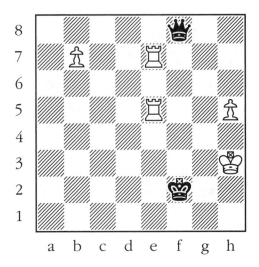

White to Move

142.

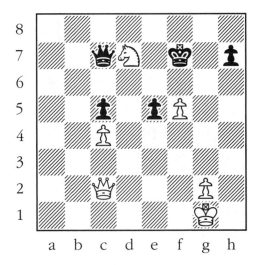

Black to Move

143.

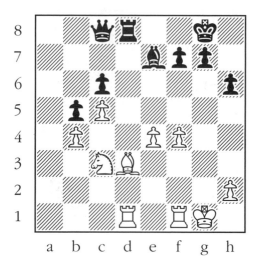

White to Move

144.

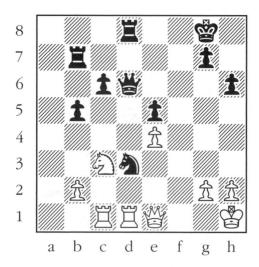

White to Move

145.

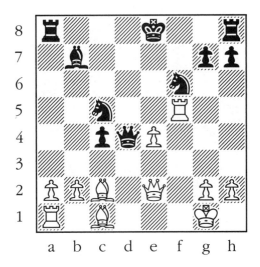

White to Move

146.

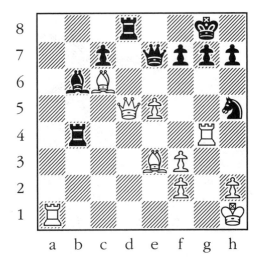

Black to Move

147.

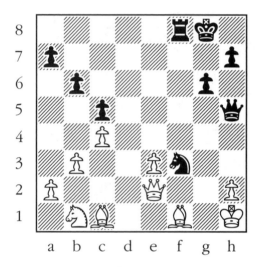

White to Move

148.

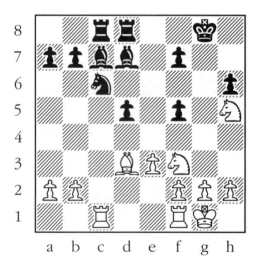

White to Move

149.

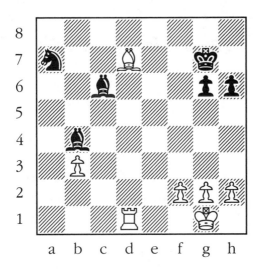

White to Move

150.

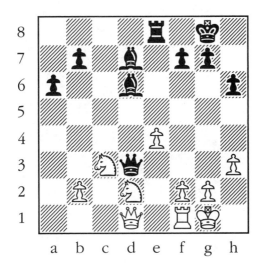

CHAPTER FOUR

THE MATING ATTACK

THE MATING ATTACK

The attack on the King is one of the cornerstones of chess strategy, since capture of the King – technical term: **checkmate** – is built into the very fabric of the rules. Carrying out the attack comes under the domain of chess tactics. Lines must be opened, defenders eliminated or neutralized, and the path to the enemy King made secure. The attack is rated completely successful when the net thrown around the King culminates in mate. But a partial success is also registered when the defender is forced to jettison material in order to save his King.

ORGANIZATION

Mating attacks depend on the tightness of the mating net. If the net holds we have a forced mate. Otherwise we just win material.

151 –165	Forced Mate in Two or Three Moves
166 –176	Forced Mate in Four or Five Moves
177 –200	Mate or Win of Material

White to Move

151.

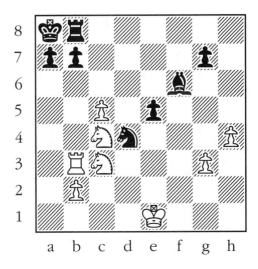

Black to Move

152.

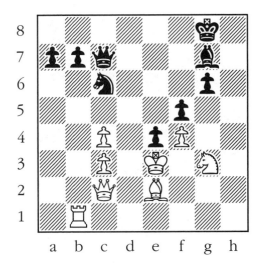

White to Move

153.

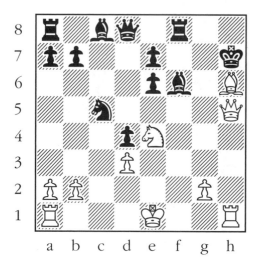

White to Move

154.

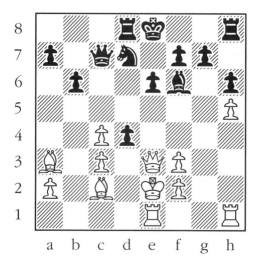

Black to Move

155.

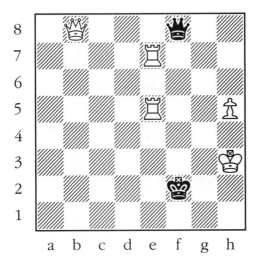

White to Move

156.

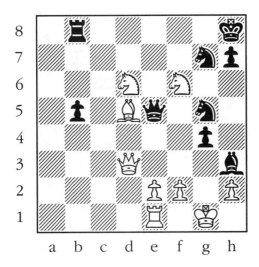

White to Move

157.

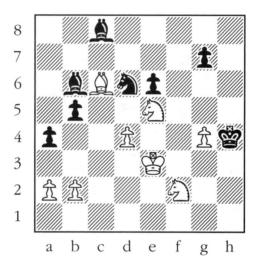

Black to Move

158.

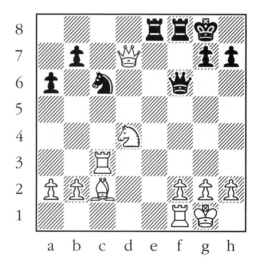

White to Move

159.

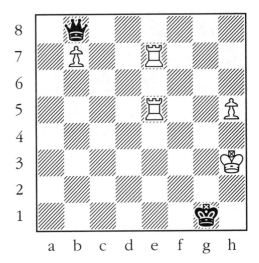

White to Move

160.

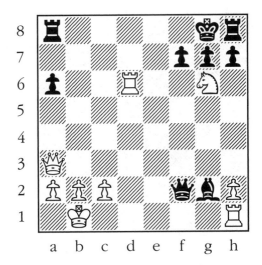

Black to Move

161.

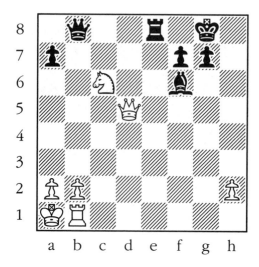

White to Move

162.

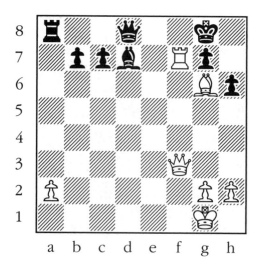

White to Move

163.

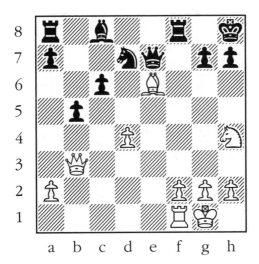

White to Move

164.

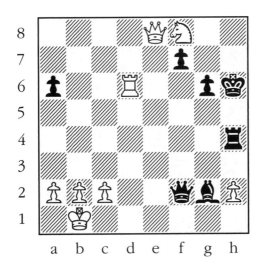

White to Move

165.

White to Move

166.

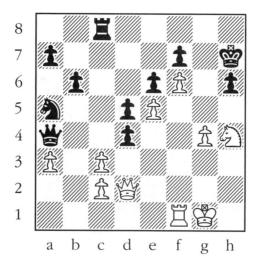

White to Move

167.

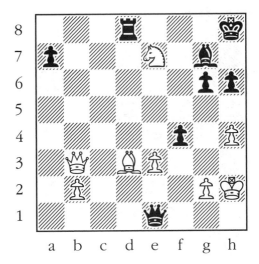

Black to Move

168.

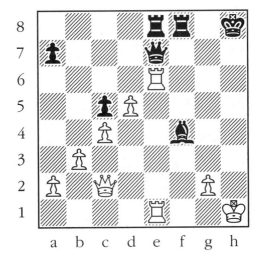

White to Move

169.

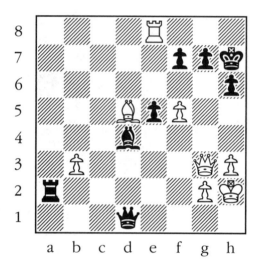

White to Move

170.

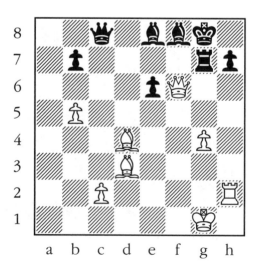

White to Move

171.

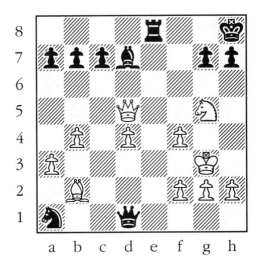

White to Move

172.

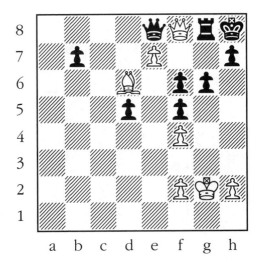

Black to Move

173.

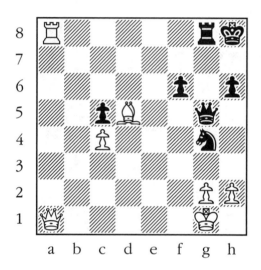

White to Move

174.

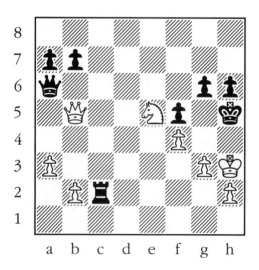

Black to Move

175.

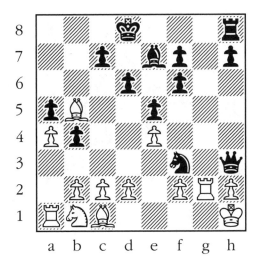

Black to Move

176.

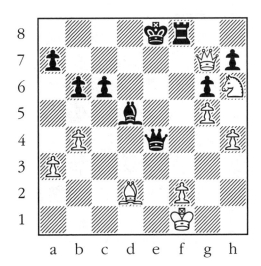

Black to Move

177.

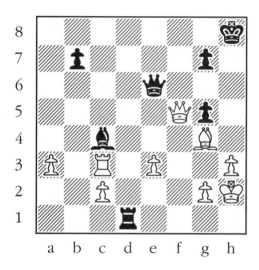

Black to Move

178.

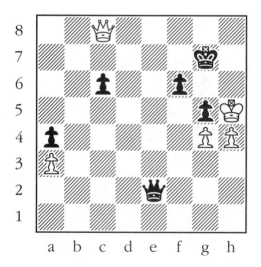

Black to Move

179.

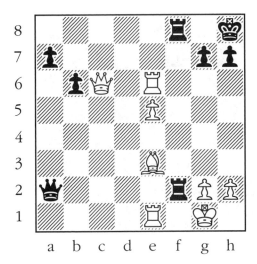

White to Move

180.

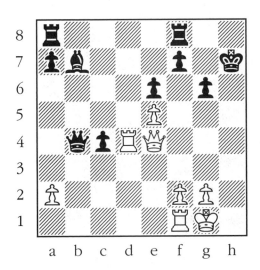

White to Move

181.

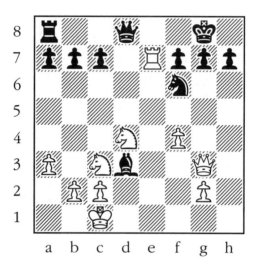

Black to Move

182.

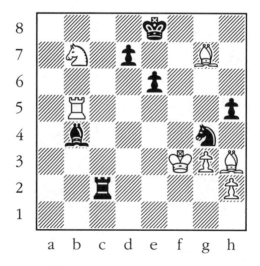

White to Move

183.

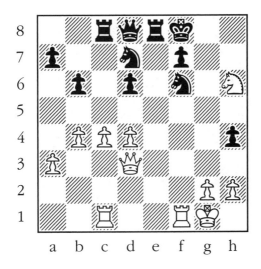

White to Move

184.

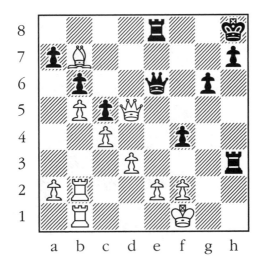

Black to Move

185.

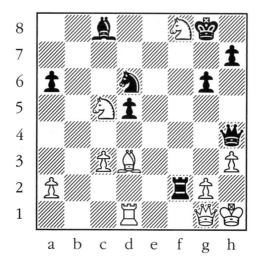

Black to Move

186.

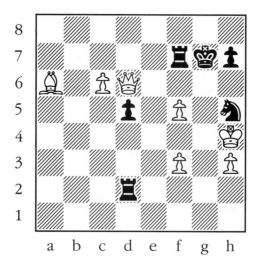

White to Move

187.

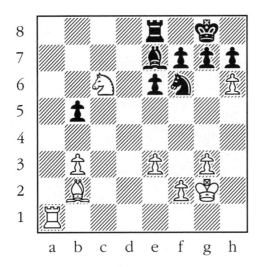

White to Move

188.

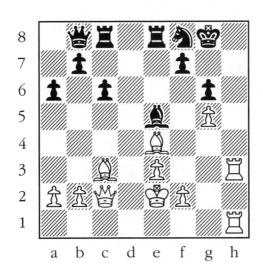

White to Move

189.

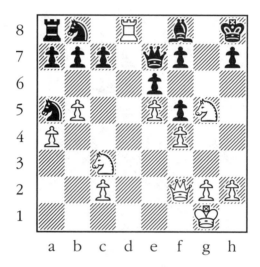

White to Move

190.

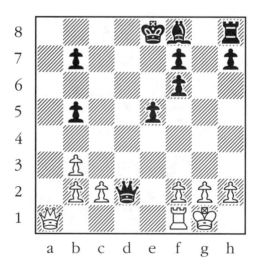

White to Move

191.

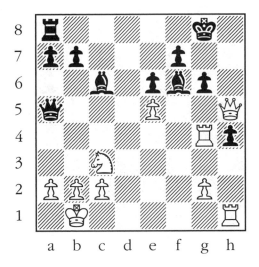

White to Move

192.

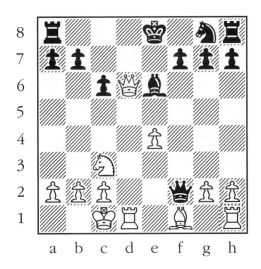

White to Move

193.

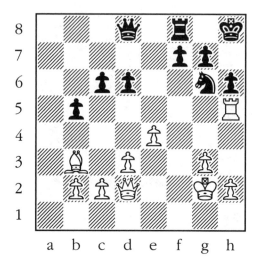

Black to Move

194.

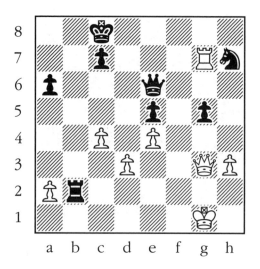

Black to Move

195.

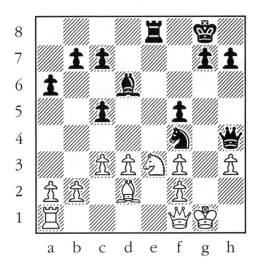

White to Move

196.

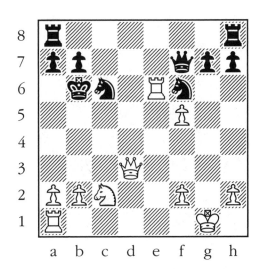

Black to Move

197.

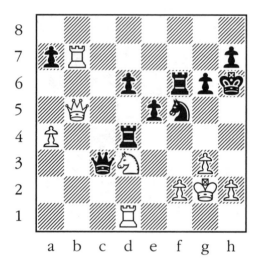

White to Move

198.

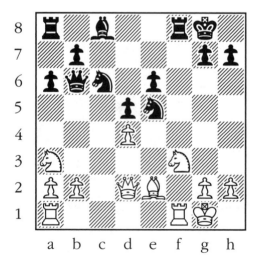

White to Move

199.

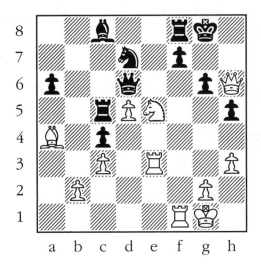

Black to Move

200.

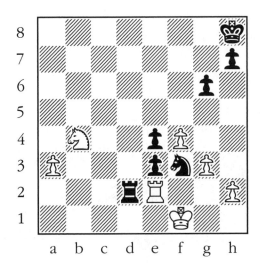

CHAPTER FIVE

UNDERMINING THE DEFENSE

UNDERMINING

In this chapter we examine the mechanism whereby the defensive structure is overthrown, or **undermined**. Here attention shifts from the primary objective to a key defender.

The annihilation theme is easy enough to grasp. The key defender is captured and removed from the board. It's called **removing the guard**. Similar in content, **driving off** is an attack on the defending unit, the intention being to drive it away from the critical sector. It's either move or be captured. A more subtle form of undermining is the **overload**, taking advantage of the situation where the defender has become overburdened with too many chores to perform. Closely related is the **deflection** sacrifice, which, like the overload, is designed to draw the defender out of position.

ORGANIZATION

Classification is by the four main undermining mechanisms.

201 – 220	Removing the Guard
221 – 230	Overload
231 – 240	Deflection
241 – 250	Driving Off

White to Move

201.

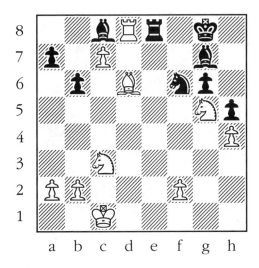

White to Move

202.

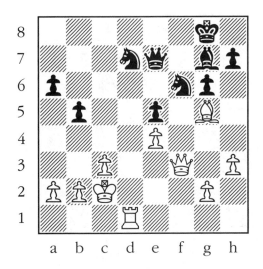

Black to Move

203.

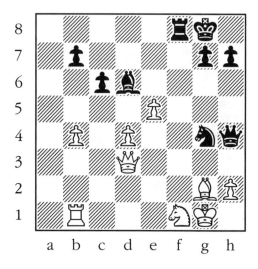

White to Move

204.

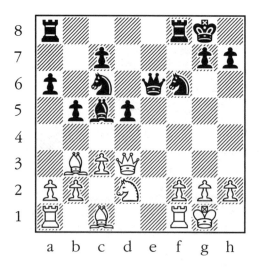

White to Move

205.

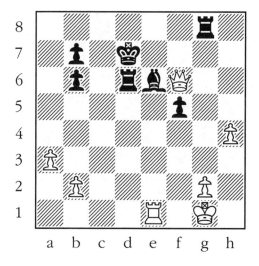

Black to Move

206.

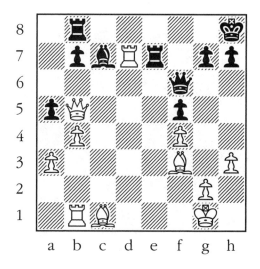

White to Move

207.

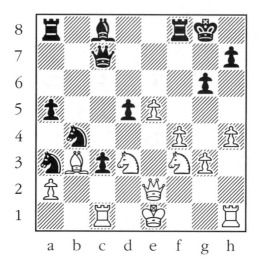

White to Move

208.

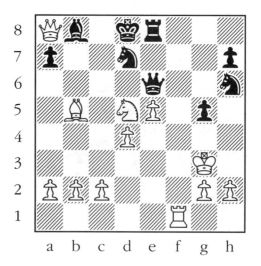

White to Move

209.

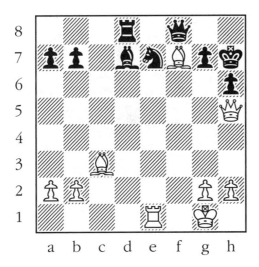

White to Move

210.

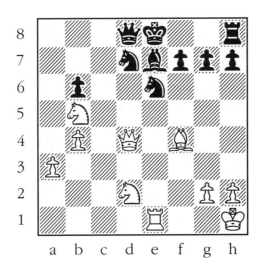

White to Move

211.

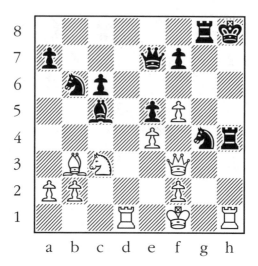

White to Move

212.

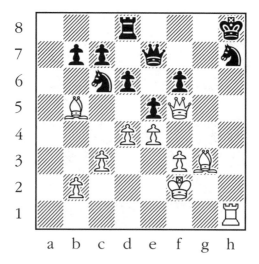

Black to Move

213.

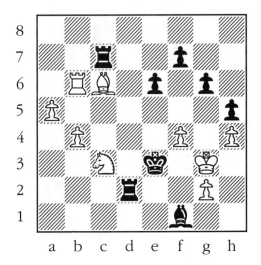

White to Move

214.

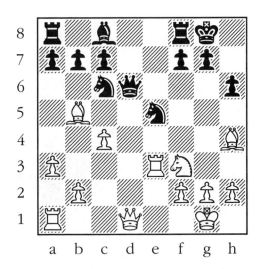

Black to Move

215.

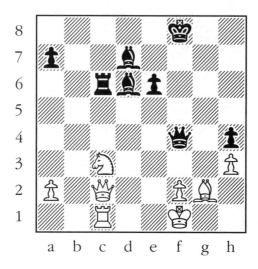

White to Move

216.

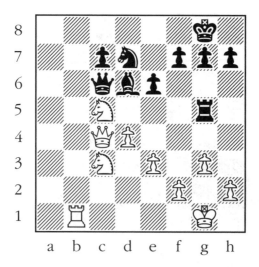

Black to Move

217.

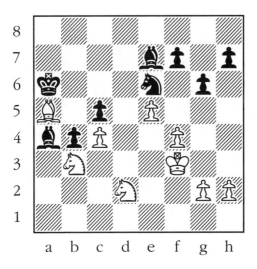

Black to Move

218.

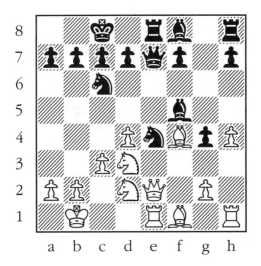

White to Move

219.

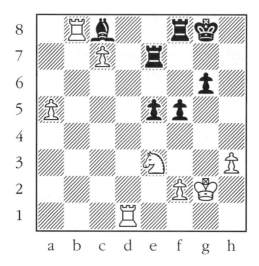

White to Move

220.

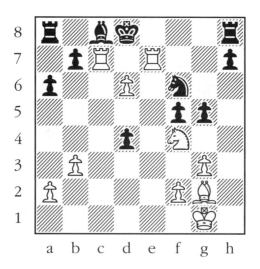

White to Move

221.

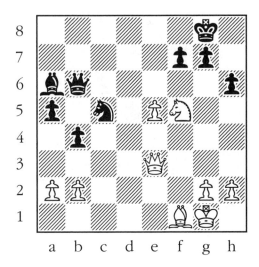

Black to Move

222.

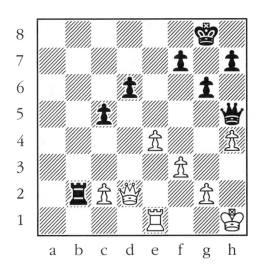

Black to Move

223.

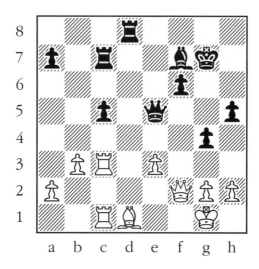

Black to Move

224.

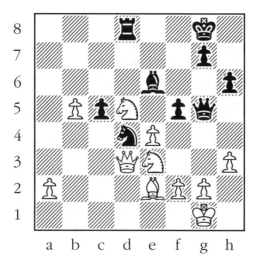

White to Move

225.

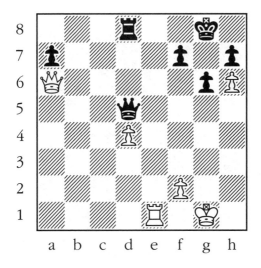

White to Move

226.

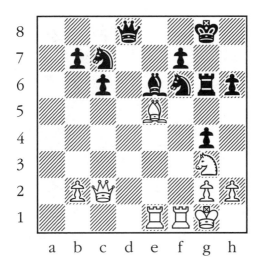

White to Move

227.

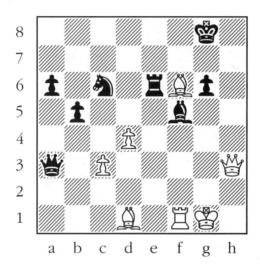

White to Move

228.

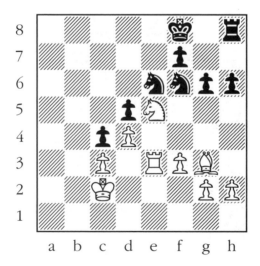

White to Move

229.

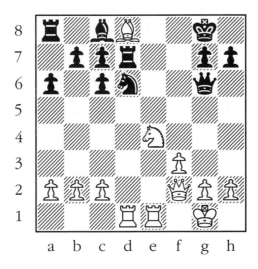

White to Move

230.

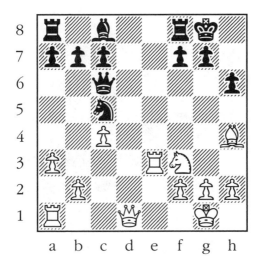

Black to Move

231.

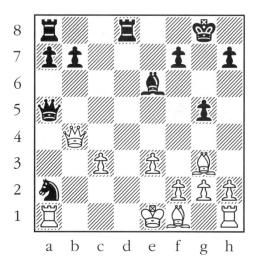

White to Move

232.

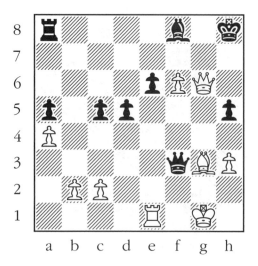

White to Move

233.

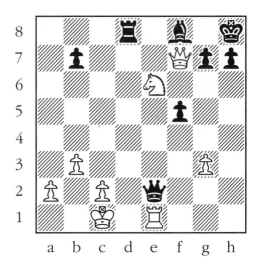

White to Move

234.

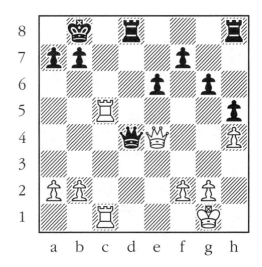

White to Move

235.

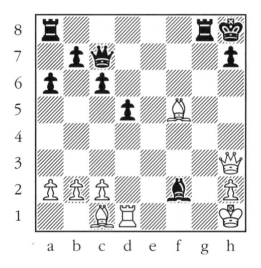

Black to Move

236.

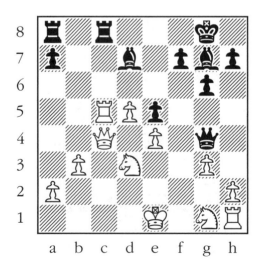

White to Move

237.

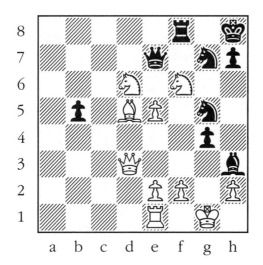

White to Move

238.

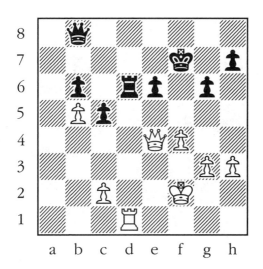

Black to Move

239.

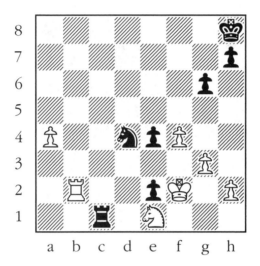

Black to Move

240.

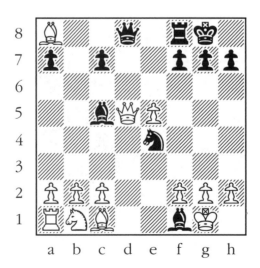

Black to Move

241.

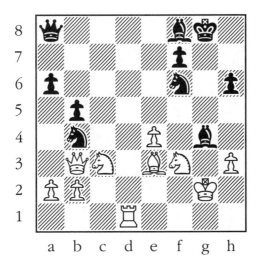

White to Move

242.

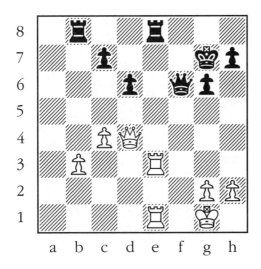

White to Move

243.

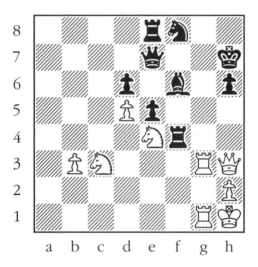

White to Move

244.

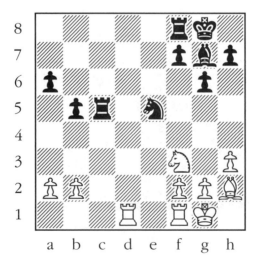

White to Move

245.

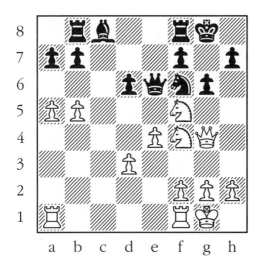

White to Move

246.

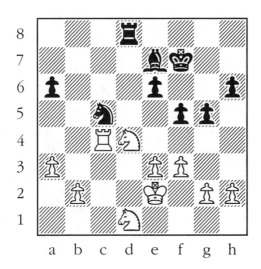

Black to Move

247.

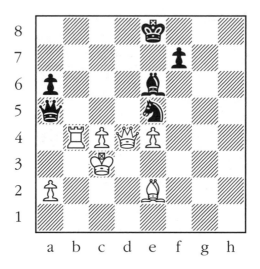

Black to Move

248.

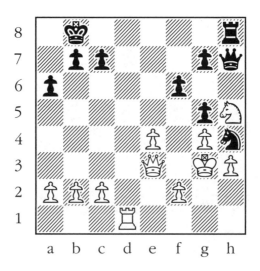

White to Move

249.

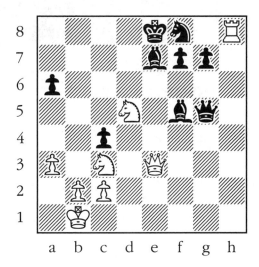

Black to Move

250.

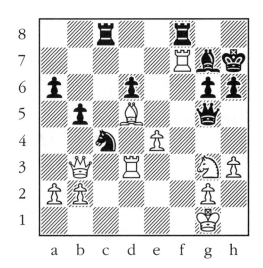

CHAPTER SIX

ASSORTED TACTICS

ASSORTED TACTICS

In this chapter we pick up a number of tactical ideas that have not previously been dealt with. The **double threat** or **double attack** is a very close relative of the fork. However, a second attacking unit is normally required in order to assist in one of the two threats.

Surrounding and attacking an enemy unit is a well-known stratagem. When it is done to the King, we call it checkmate. When it's done to any other unit, it's called **trapping**.

The endgame and for that matter, the latter stages of the middle game, carry with them their own special themes. Pawn **promotion**, the appearance of a new Queen on the board, is certain to upset the material balance in a decisive way.

And finally, a player facing imminent defeat must pull out all the stops to try and salvage a draw. Coming to his rescue are the very rules of the game which permit draw by **stalemate** and three fold repetition of position. **Perpetual check** falls under the repetition rule.

Salvation may also be obtained by reaching a known endgame where the superior side simply does not have enough power on the board to enforce checkmate. This is called the **book draw**.

ORGANIZATION

The grouping of positions is by the four main themes mentioned above.

251 – 262	Double Threat
263 – 274	Trapping
275 – 286	Promotion
287 – 303	Draw: Stalemate, Perpetual, Book Draw

White to Move

251.

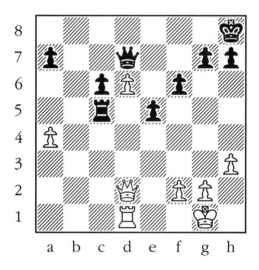

White to Move

252.

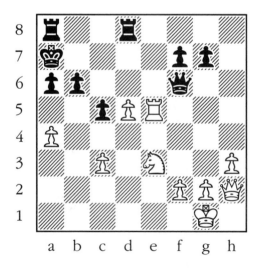

White to Move

253.

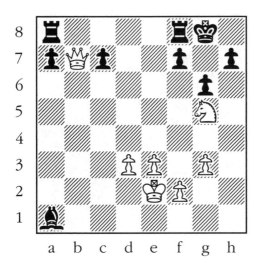

Black to Move

254.

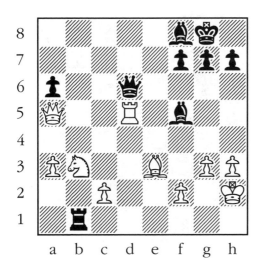

Black to Move

255.

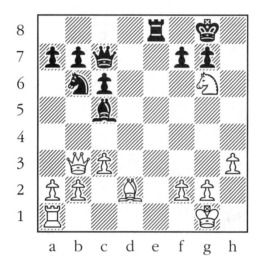

Black to Move

256.

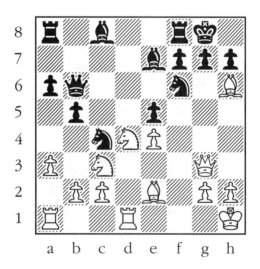

Black to Move

257.

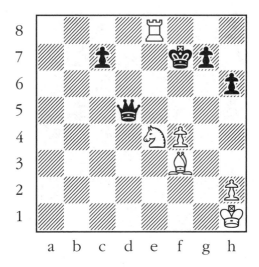

White to Move

258.

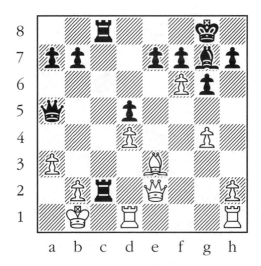

Black to Move

259.

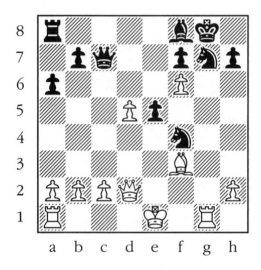

White to Move

260.

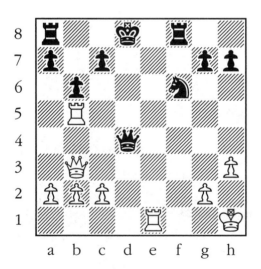

White to Move

261.

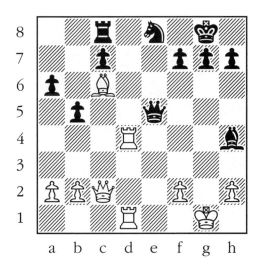

White to Move

262.

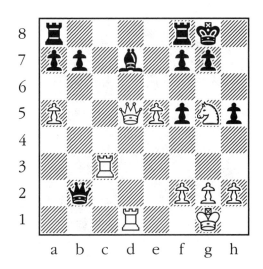

Black to Move

263.

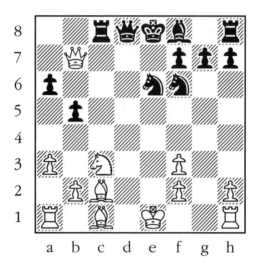

White to Move

264.

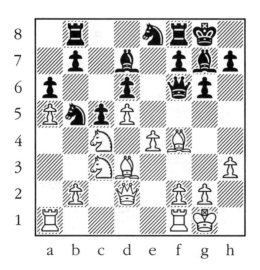

White to Move

265.

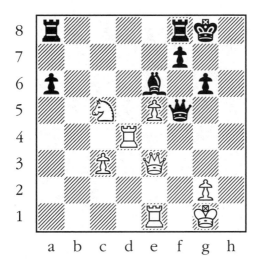

White to Move

266.

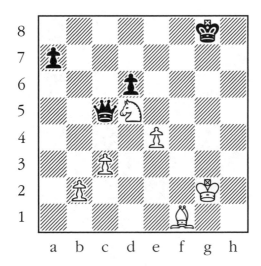

Black to Move

267.

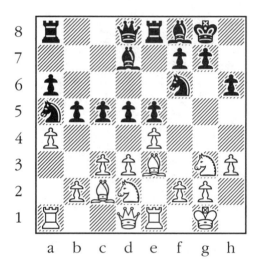

White to Move

268.

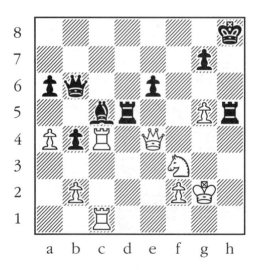

White to Move

269.

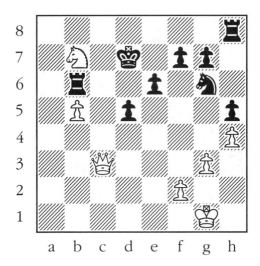

White to Move

270.

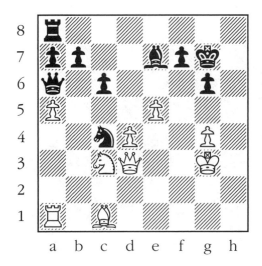

Black to Move

271.

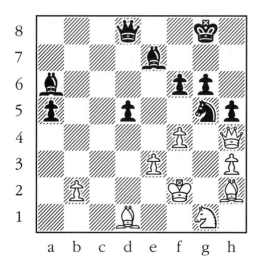

White to Move

272.

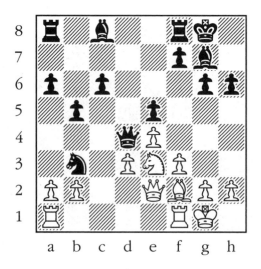

White to Move

273.

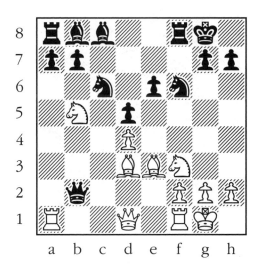

Black to Move

274.

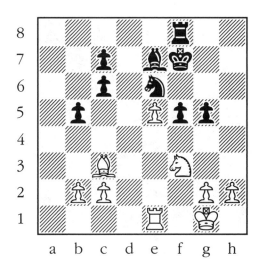

White to Move

275.

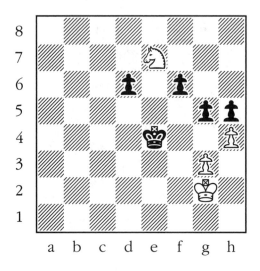

Black to Move

276.

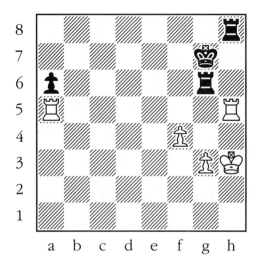

Black to Move

277.

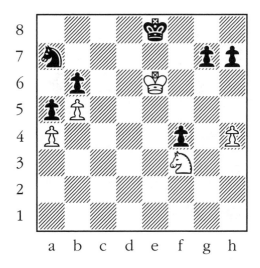

White to Move

278.

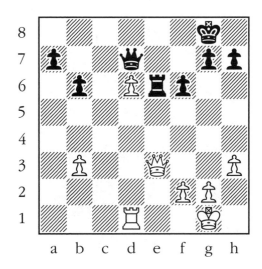

White to Move

279.

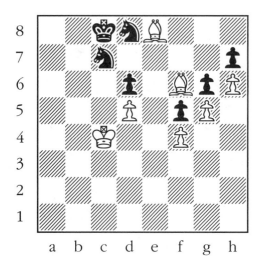

Black to Move

280.

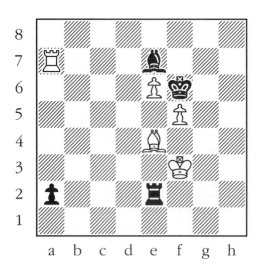

Black to Move

281.

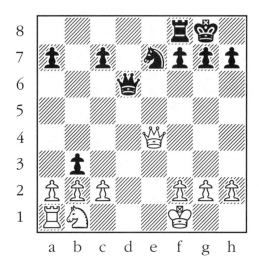

Black to Move

282.

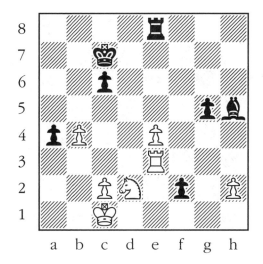

White to Move

283.

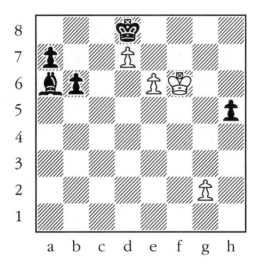

White to Move

284.

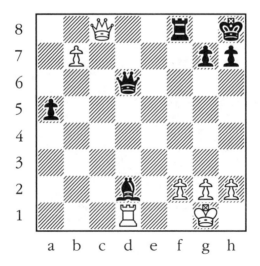

White to Move

285.

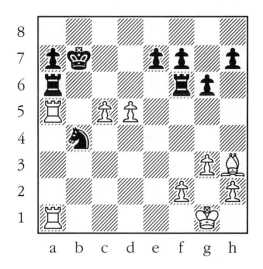

Black to Move

286.

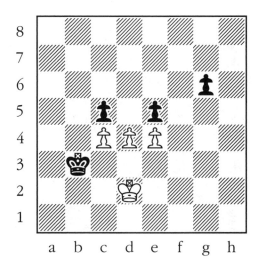

White to Move

287.

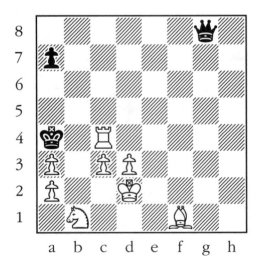

Black to Move

288.

White to Move

289.

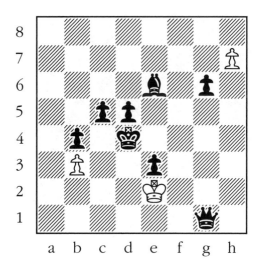

Black to Move

290.

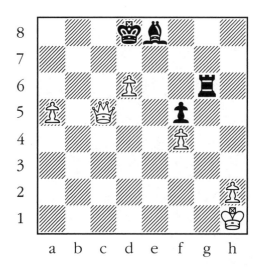

Black to Move

291.

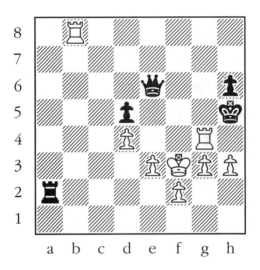

White to Move

292.

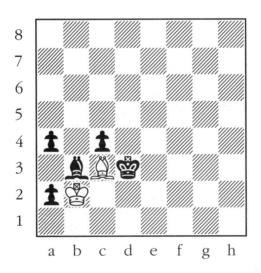

White to Move

293.

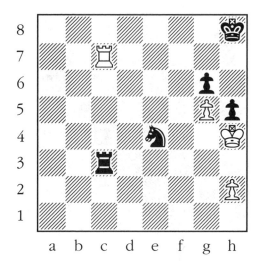

White to Move

294.

White to Move

295.

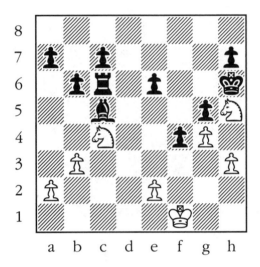

White to Move

296.

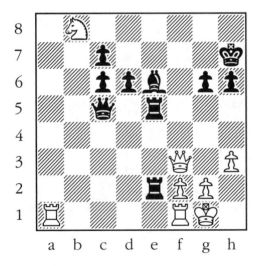

White to Move

297.

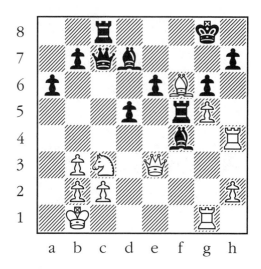

Black to Move

298.

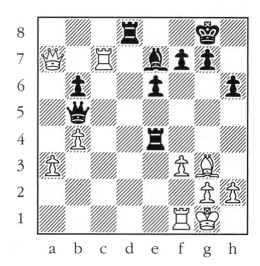

White to Move

299.

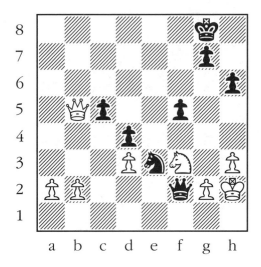

Black to Move

300.

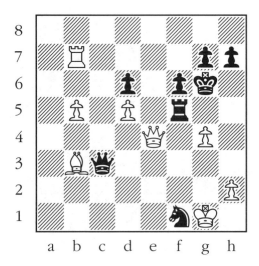

Black to Move

301.

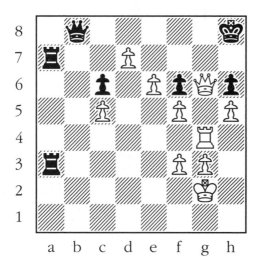

White to Move
302.

White to Move
303.

SOLUTIONS

#1 **1...Nb3** *wins the exchange one way or another. If the Queen moves, then* **2...Nxa1**, *and if* **2.axb3 Qxa1+**

#2 **1.Ng6+ Kg7** (**1...Nxg6** *allows* **2.Rxh7#**) **2.Nxe7** *wins a piece.*

#3 **1...Rxf2+ 2.Kxf2 Ne4+ 3.Kf1 Nxg5** *gains material and Black still has the attack..*

#4 **1...Bxf2+ 2.Kxf2 Ne4+** *and* **3...Nxc3** *gains the Queen.*

#5 **1.Qxf5 Qxf5 2.Ne7+** *and* **3.Nxf5** *wins a full Rook.*

#6 **1.Qxc6 Qxc6 2.Ne7+** *and* **3.Nxc6** *picks up a piece.*

#7 **1.Qh6+ Ke8** (*or* **1...Kg8 2.Qg7#**) **2.Ng7+** *and* **3.Nxe6** *wins the Queen.*

#8 **1.Nd6+ Kf8 2.Nxe6+ Kg8 3.Nxc7** *leaves White with three pieces for a Rook. Black should cough up the Queen right away with* **1...Qxd6 2.exd6**, *but of course White is still ahead.*

#9 **1.Nf6** *wins the house. The Knight attacks h5, d5, and threatens* **Rxh7**.*It's too much.*

#10 **1...Qh1+ 2.Kxh1 Nxf2+ 3.Kg2 Nxd3 4.cxd3** *simplifies to an easily winning King and Pawn ending. After all, Black is a pawn up.*

#11 **1.Rxg7+ Kxg7 2.Nxe6+ Kf7 3.Nxc7** *picks up two pawns. The Knight will escape trapping by* **4.e4** *and* **5.Nd5**.

#12 **1...Nf4** *wins the exchange. White could try to get fancy with* **2.Nf6+ gxf6 3.Bxh7+** *but* **3...Kh8!** *collapses the attack. Hope you saw* **3...Kh8** *because everything else loses.*

#13 **1.Rxb7 Qxb7 2.Qf7+ Kc8 3.Nd6+** *wins the Queen.*

#14 **1...Bxc2 2.Qxc2 Rxf3** *wins a piece. And if* **3.Kxf3? Nxd4+** *and* **4...Nxc2** *wins the Queen.*

#15 **1...Rxb4 2.Rxb4 e1/Q+ 3.Kxe1 Nc2+** *and* **4...Nxb4** *leaves Black with a piece for a pawn. He should be able to win the ending.*

#16 **1.Bxg6+ Kxg6 2.Qf5+ Kg7 3.Ne6+** *and* **4.Nxc7** *wins the Queen.*

#17 **1...Re2** (A)**2.Qxe2 Nc3+** *and* **3... Nxe2** (B)**2.Qg1 Nc3+ 3.Kc1 Nxd1 4.Qxd1 Re1** *wins the Queen.*

#18 **1...Qxa3+ 2.Kxa3 a1/Q+ 3.Qxa1 Nxc2+** *and* **4...Nxa1** *with a winning King and Pawn ending.*

#19 *Black untraps his Knight by* **1...**
Rxc3.2.bxc3 Ne2+
followed by **3...Nxg1** *and then
picking up the e5-pawn.*

#20 **1.Ng5** (*threatens* **2.Nxe6+** *or*
2.Nh7+) **1...Qe8 2.Nxe6+**
Ke7 3.Qxe8+ Kxe8 4.Nc7+
and **5.Nxa6** *winning a Bishop.*

#21 **1...Rd1+ 2.Kh2 Qb8+** *and
Black wins the Rook.*

#22 **1.Nxf7 Rxf7 2.Qxg6+** *and*
3.Qxd3 *picks up two pawns.*

#23 **1...Bxe2** *wins a clear pawn.
For if* **2.Rxe2? Qd3** *forks both
White Rooks.*

#24 **1...Qf5+** *wins the
f6-Knight. If* **2.Ne4?** *then* **2...**
Nd2+! *wins the Queen.*

#25 **1.Nf6+ gxf6 2.Qg4+** *and*
3.Qxd7 *wins the exchange.*

#26 **1...Rgf3+ 2.Ke1 Qg1+**
3.Kd2 Qxh1 *puts Black ahead.*

#27 **1...Rxa1+ 2.Bxa1 Bxg2+**
3.Kxg2 Qa8+ *and* **4...Qxa1**
wins a pawn.

#28 **1.Rxf8+ Qxf8 2.Qxg6+ Kh8**
(**2...Qg7 3.Rb8+**)
3.Qh5+ *and* **4.Qxe2**.

#29 **1.Bb5+ c6 2 . Bxc6+ bxc6**
3.Qxc6+ *followed by taking the
a8-Rook with check and then clean-
ing up on e3.Net gain–the exchange
and a couple of pawns.*

#30 **1.Bxf5 exf5 2.Qf3 Ne7**
3.Qh3 Ng6 4.Qxf5 *wins a
pawn.*

#31 **1...Nf2+ 2.Kg1 Nh3+**
3.Kg2 Qe4+ (*or* **3...Qc2+**)
4.Kxh3 Qxb1, *regaining the exchange and leaving Black with a won
Queen and Pawn ending. Black has
two extra pawns.*

#32 **1...Bxd4+** *and* **2...Bxa1**
garners a Rook. White cannot afford
2.Nxd4?? Qe1#

#33 **1...Bc4+** *wins the a6-Rook. If*
2.Rxc4? *then* **2...Rb1+** *leads to a
back row mate.*

#34 **1...Rxd6 2.Rxd6 Be5** *and* **3...**
Bxg3 *gains two pieces for a Rook.
It's usually enough to win.*

#35 **1.Rxd7 Qxd7** (**1...Qxc4?**
2.Qxg7#) **2.Bxe6+** *forks King
and Queen.*

#36 **1...e3 2.fxe3 Bxe3+**
3.Rxe3 (*else* **3...Bxd2**) **3...**
Rxe3 *wins the exchange.*

#37 **1...Rxb2 2.Rxb2 Bxc3**
3.Qc1 Qd4+ *and* **4...Bxb2.**

#38 **1.Nxc5 dxc5 2.d6 Bxd6**
3.Bxb7 *forks both Rooks and wins
the exchange.*

#39 **1.Nxe4 Rxe4 2.Nxc6** *and if*
2...bxc6? 3.Bxc6 *snares one of
Black's Rooks.*

#40 **1.Ne6+ Rxe6 2.dxe6 Bxe3**
3.Qxe3 *and if* **3...Bxe6?**
4.Bxe5+ *wins the Queen.*

#41 **1.Qd2+ Kh7 2.Rd7+** *wins the Queen.*

#42 **1.Ne5 Qxe2** (*if* **1...Qf5**
2.g4 *drives off the Queen*)
2.Re3 *forking Queen and Bishop.*

#43 **1...Rxe4** *forks Queen and Knight and sets things up. If* **2.Nxe4 Rxd1+** *wins the Queen. And if* **2.Qxe4 Qxd1+** *followed by* **3...Rxd2** *wins the Knight.*

#44 **1.Bxe5 Rd8 (1...Bxe5? 2.Rc8+) 2.Bxf6 gxf6 3.Rc6** *and White gains two pawns.*

#45 **1...Ndxe5 2.Bxe5 Bxb1 3.Nxb1 Rd1+** *and* **4...Rxb1**

#46 **1...e1/Q+ 2.Kxe1 Nf3+ 3.Kd1 Rd2+ 4.Kc1 Rxd5** *winning a Knight. If White varies with* **3.Kf1**, *he runs into* **3... Nd2+** *forking King and Rook. Black can also stop for* **3... Nxh2+** *since* **4.Kg1 Nf3+ 5.Kh1?? Rh2** *is mate.*

#47 **1...Qxf3 2.exf3 f5** *gathers in one of the White Knights.*

 # 48 **1.d4 Bxd4 2.Bf4** *wins another piece while breaking Black's attack. If* **2...Qg6 3.Ne7+** *and if* **2... Qg4 3.Bh3. So 2...Qf2+ 3.Qxf2 Bxf2 3.Kxf2** *and White is still winning.*

#49 **1...Qd3+ 2.Qxd3 exd3** *and the c2-Knight is lost. If the Knight tries to move, say* **3.Nb4**, *then* **3...d2** *forks both White Rooks.*

#50 **1.d6**
(A)**1...cxd6 2.Bxd6** *forks b8-Rook and e7-Knight.*
(B)**1...Nc6 2.Qb3+! Kh8 3.dxc7** *wins.*

(C)**1...gxf4 2.dxe7 Qxd1 3.exf8/Q+ Kxf8 4.Raxd1** *wins.*

#51 **1...Bxe3** *exploits the double pin. Black is sure to win something, either the c1-Rook or the f4-Bishop.*

#52. **1.Kd1** *followed by* **2.Re1** *pinning the Queen, or* **2.Qxh8** *winning the Rook.*

#53. **1...Rf3** *followed up with* **2... Rxf4+** *and* **3...Bxg5** *wins a Knight.*

#54. **1.Nxf6** *threatens* **2.N(x)d7+.** *And if* **1...Qxf6 2.Re7+ K-moves 3.Qxf6** *wins the Queen.*

#55 **1.Rh7+ Ke8 2.Bb5** *and wins the pinned Queen.*

#56 **1.Rf1 e4 (or 1...Qd6) 2.g5** *piles on and wins the Knight.*

#57 *Faced with a mate threat at f2, White extricates with* **1.Rxg7+** *and* **2.Rg1** *nabbing Black's Queen and breaking the attack.*

#58 **1.Qxe5 dxe5 2.Rxd7** *regains the Queen, finishing with an extra Bishop.*

#59 **1.g4+ Rxg4 2.Qf3** *and* **3.Qxg4** *is pretty straightforward.*

#60 **1...axb2+ 2.Rxb2+ Ka3** *and* **3...Bxb2** *will be mate.*

#61 *The right way is* **1.Qc8+ Qe8 (1...Kg7 2.Rd7) 2.Qxc7** *winning a piece. The* *wrong way is* **1.Rd7? Re1+ 2.Ng1 Rxg1+ 3.Kxg1 Qe1** *and Black mates.*

#62 **1.Qh5+ Kd8** (*if* **1...g6** *then* **2.Bxg6+**) **2.Ba5** *confiscates the Queen.*

#63 **1...Rxf3 2.Rxf3 Qe2+ 3.Qf2 Bxf3+** *exploits the double pin to win a piece.*

#64. *Hooray for the counterpin.*
1.Ra8!
(A)**1...Rxa8 2.Qxa8+Kg7 3.Qf8#**
(B)**1...Qg5 2.Rxd8+ Bxd8 3.Rf8+** *winning the Bishop.*
(C)**1...Bb8 2.Rxb8 Rxb8 3.Qe5+** *and* **4.Qxb8+**

#65 **1.Nxc5** *wins a piece. For if* **1... Rxc5? 2.Qa3!** *followed by* **3.Rxc5 and 4.Rc1** *wins a Rook.*

#66 *Black piles up on the pinned Knight by* **1...Bf8 2.Re2 Bb4 3.Re3 Nc2** *gaining a full piece.*

#67 **1...Qh3+ 2.Qh2 Qf3+ 3.Rg2 h3** *wins the g2-Rook.*

#68 **1.Bg6 Qxf6** (*else the White Queen mates at h7 or g7*) **2.Qh7+ Kf8 3.Rf1** *catches the Queen in a pin.*

#69 **1...Qxg2+ 2.Qxg2 Rxf1+ 3.Bg1** *and now* **3...Kxf7** *seems simplest, when Black emerges with an extra Rook after taking the Queen.*

#70 **1.Bxf6 Bxf6 2.Bd5 Qc7 3.Qxf6** *followed by* **4.Qxf7** *wins a full Rook.*

#71 **1.gxf5 exf4 2.c5 N-moves 3.c6** *wins the Bishop.*

#72 *The double pin enables White to make off first with the Queen and later the King:*
1.Qxf6 Kh8 (*else* **2.Qxg7#**) **2.Rh5+ Kg8 3.Qg6** *and mate next at f7 or h7.*

#73 *The basic idea is* **1.Qf8+ Qxf8 2.Rxf8+ Kh7 3.Bd3** *winning the Rook. And* **1...Kh7** *comes to much the same after* **2.Bg8+ Kh8** (**2... Kg6 3.Qf5#**) **3.Be6+ Qxf8 4.Rxf8+ Kh7 5.Bf5+** *and* **6.Bxe4.**

#74 **1.Bd1 Rg7** (*to stop mate*) **2.fxg4+ Rxg4 3.Rf6** *followed by* **4.Rf5+** *and* **5.Bxg4.** *Compare with #53.*

#75 **1.Bxf5** *wins a clear pawn. Black cannot afford* **1...exf5? 2.Rfe1 Be6 3.Rxe6 Qxe6 4.Re1** *pinning and winning.*

#76 **1.Rc3+ Kd8** (**1...Kb8 2.Nd7+ Ka8 3.Rc8#**) **2.Rd3 Ke7 3.Rxd5 Kd6 4.Ng4 Rf1+ 5.Rd1** *and keeps his hard won piece.*

#77 *The combination starts with* **1... Nxd4 2.Nxd4 Bc5,** *pinning to set things up. After* **3.c3** *Black continues* **3...Qf6+ 4.Qf3** (**4.Kg1? Rxd4!**) **4... Bxd4+ 5.cxd4 Qxd4+ 6.Kf1 Qxb2** *forking Rook and Bishop.*

#78 **1... Bxc5+** *forces* **2.bxc5** *when* **2...Qxf4** *picks off the Queen.*

#79   **1.Qe1** *holds the Rook in place. Then* **2.b4** *drives off the defending Queen to allow* **3.Qxd2**, *winning the Rook in broad daylight.*

#80   **1.Qb4** *and Black falls apart. If* **1...Rd8** *(what else?) then* **2.Qxf8+ Rxf8 3.Rxb6** *looks simplest.*

#81   **1...Nxe5 2.Nxe5 Qd6** *recovers the piece, winning a pawn.*

#82   **1.Nxd7+ Nxd7 2.Qxe6+** *and* **3.Rxd7**

#83   **1...0-0-0 2.Be3 Bb4+ 3.Bd2 Bxd2+** *and* **4...Nxd4** *wins a Knight.*

#84   **1.e6 fxe6 2.Ne5 Rf4 3.g3!** **(3.Nxd7? Qh4** *gets messy)* **3... Rf7 4.Nxf7** *wins the exchange.*

#85   **1...Bh6!**
(A)**2.Rxh4 Bxg5**
(B)**2.Bxh4 Bxd2+**
(C)**2.Bxd8 Bxd2+ 3.Kxd2 Rxh1 4.Nxh1 Kxd8**
(D)**2.Bxh6 Rxh1 3.Nxh1** **(3.Bg5 Rxf1+ 4.Kxf1 f6) 3...Qh4+ 4.Nf2 Qxh6** *and Black keeps his extra pawn. It's a lot of work just to retain a pawn.*

#86   **1...Nb4+**
(A)**2.cxb4 Bxa1**
(B)**2.Kd1 Qxa1+**
(C)**2.Kb1 Rxe1+**
(D)**2.Kb2 Nxd3+ 3.Bxd3 Bxc3+ 4.Kxc3 Qxd3+ 5.Kb4 Rb6+ 6.Ka3 Ra6+ 7.Kb4 (7.Kb2 Qc2#) 7... Rxa1 8.Rxa1 Qd4+** *and* **9... Qxa1.**

#87   **1...Nb4+ 2.cxb4** *(forced)* **2... Rxh3**

88   **1...Nb3** *takes advantage of the pinned a2-pawn* **(2.axb3 Rxa1)** *to win the Rook in the corner.*

#89   **1.Ra8+!** *(not* **1.Ra7 Re1+** *and the Knight can move away)* **1... Kg7 2.Ra7** *wins a piece. If* **2... Re1+ 3Kh2** *and the Knight is still pinned.*

#90   **1...Rxc3** *wins a pawn. If* **2.bxc3 Qxb1+** *and if* **2.Qxc3 Bb4** *pins the Queen.*

#91   **1.Qxd3 e4 2.Qe2** *pins the e-pawn* **(2....exf3? 3.Qxe8+)** *and White remains ahead two pieces for a Rook.*

#92   **1...Rxc4 2.Rxc4 Bxc4** *wins a pawn and more if White goes for* **3.bxc4? Rxb1.** *Note that* **1... Bxc4?** *allows White to turn the tables with* **2.Rc1!**

#93   **1.Nxb6 cxb6 2.Rxc8+ Rxc8 3.Rxc8+ Bxc8 4.Qxc8+** *wins a pawn.*

#94   **1.Nxb6 cxb6 2.Qxa6 Rxa6 3.Rxc8+ Kf7 4.R1c7** *regains the Queen and wins a pawn.*

#95   **1.Qd8+ Kf7 2.Qc7+ Ke6 3.Qc6+! Ke5 4.b4 Be3 5.Qe8+** *wins the Bishop.*

#96   **1...Bh3** *wins the Queen or else mates after* **2.Qxg5? Rf1#**

#97   **1...Bh5** *wins a piece as* **2.Bxh5? Qxh2+ 3.Kf1 Qh1** *or* **Qf2** *is mate.*

#98   **1.Bd3** *and if the Rook on f5 moves, then* **2.Rh8+ Nh7 3.Rxh7#**

177

#99 **1.Bxh7+ Nxh7 2.Rch1** *and if Knight moves then* **3.Rh8#**

#100 **1.Rxe7 Nxe7? 2.Qxh7+ Kf8 3.Qh8+ Ng8 4.Qxg7+ Ke8 5.Qf7#**

#101 **1.Nd5** *threatens* **2.Qf8#** *and the c7-Rook. Also,* **1.Nc6** *hitting the Queen with threat of mate.*

#102 **1.Ngf6+ gxf6 2.Bxf5** *wins the Queen.*

#103 **1...Nd3+ 2.Kf1 Rxd8** *wins a piece.*

#104 **1.Nh6+ Kh8 2.Qxd7**

#105 **1...Bxf2+ 2.Kxf2 Ng4+** *and* **3...Qxg5.**

#106 **1...Nd3+ (A) 2.Kxe2 Rxb2+** *and* **3...Ra2**
(B) 2.Kg2 Rxb2 3.a8/Q+ Kg7 *and the Black e2-pawn Queens shortly.*

#107 *The idea is* **1...Ne4 2.Rb1 Nc3 3.Qc2 Nxb1** *winning the exchange. White might try* **2.d4,** *closing the diagonal, but it costs at least a pawn.*

#108 **1.Nd6+ Rxd6+ 2.cxd6** *and if* **2...Bxf3 3.d7** *promotes.*

#109 **1.Nd6 (A) 1...Nxd6 2.Qg5#**
(B) 1...Rxd8 2.Nxf7
(C)1...Qf6 2.Qxf6+ Kxf6 3.Ne4+ *and* **4.Rxa8**

#110 **1.Ne7+ Bxe7 2.Bxe6+ Rf7 3.Qxf7+ Kh8 4.Qh5#**
A little overlap. The discovery leads to a mating net.

#111 **1.Rb8+**
(A)1...Kh7 2.Rh8+ Kg6 3.Ne5+ Kf5 4.e4+ Kf6 5.Nd3+ e5 6.Bxe5+ Ke6 7.Rh6+ Kd7 8.Nxc1
(B)1...Kf7 2.Ne5+ Kf6 3.Nd3+ e5 4.Bxe5+ Ke6 5.Nxc1 Kxe5 6.Rxb4 Bxb4 7.Nd3+ *and* **8.Nxb4**

#112 **1...Bg1!** *threatens* **2...Qxh2#** *as well as* **2...Rxd3.**

#113 **1...Bh2+ 2.Kxh2 Rxe1.**

#114 **1...Nxd5 2.Qxd5 Bb5** *wins material. Also* **1...Bb5** *immediately works:* **2.Nxf6+ Bxf6 3.Ng3 Bxf1** *winning the exchange.*

#115 **1...Qd8!** *retains the extra piece. For if* **2.Kxe2?** *then* **2...Ba6+** *and* **3...Qxa8.**

#116 **1.Bb5+**
(A)1...c6 2.Qxd8#
(B)1...Bd7 2.Bxf6 gxf6 3.Qxd7+ *wins a piece.*
(C)1...Ke7 2.Qb4+ *wins the Queen.*

#117 *Not* **1...Nxc1? 2.Qf7+ Kh8 3.Qf8+** *and mate next move. Nor* **1...Qe6? 2.Kxe2 Bb8+ 3.Re3** *and White wins. But* **1... Qe8! 2.Kxe2 Bb8+ 3.Re3 Qb5+** *and* **4...Bxa7** *winning.*

#118 **1.e6 f6** *(else* **2.Be5+)* **2.Bf8 Rxf8 3.Rxd8 Rxd8 4.e7** *wins. If* **4...Re8** *then* **5.Qf8+**

#119 **1.Bxc4 Qxd7 2.Bxf7+ Kf8 3.Bxb3+ Bf6 4.Rxf6+ Kg7**

5.Rf7+ (*double check*) **5...Kh6
6. Rxd7 Rxe5
7.Bd5** *and White wins easily.*

#120 **1...Rc3+ 2.Kd2 Rd3+** *and*
3...Rxd4 *wins a Knight.*

#121 **1...Bb5** (*threatens* **2...Rc1+**)
2.Kg2 Rc2 (*threatens* **3...f1/
Q+**). *It's two too many discoveries.
White has no defence.*

#122 **1...Rxf2** (*much better than* **1...
Bxf2+ 2.Kf1**). *Now Black
threatens mainly* **2...Rf3+
3.Kh1 Rf1#**
So, **2.g3** (*or* **2.Nc2 Rxc2+**)
2...Rf7+ *and* **3...Rxd7**

#123 **1...Rc2+** *and White has to let
the Knight go. If* **2.Kd1** *Black
discovers with* **2...Rc7+** *and* **3...
Rxh7** *picks up the Rook.*

#124 **1.Re7+ (A) 1...Kf8 2.Bg7+
Kg8 3.Nf6# (B) 1...Kd8
2.Rh7+ Ke8 (2...Kc8
3.Rxh8+** *and* **4.Rxa8)
3.Nc7+ Kf8 4.Ne6+** *and Rook
mates on g7 or e7.*

#125 **1...Rxc4 2.Qxc4 b5** *and Black
collects the a7-Bishop with* **3...
Qxa7.**

#126 **1...Rxe4+ 2.Kxe4 f2+** *and*
3...f1/Q

#127 **1.d7+ Ka8 2.Rc8+ Rxc8
3.dxc8/Q#**

#128 **1.dxe6 Bxf4 2.e7+ Bf7
3.Qxd8**

#129 **1...Rf2** (*threatens mate at g2 or
h2*) **2.Qxf2 e3+ 3.Kg1 exf2+**
and wins.

#130 **1.Rxg7+ Kxg7 2.e6+ Bf6**
(*else* **3.Qf7** *is mate*)
**3.Qf7+ Kh6 4.Qxf6+ Kh5
5.Qxf5+ Kh6 6.Be3+ Kg7
7.Qf7+ Kh8 8.Bd4#**

#131 **1.Qh4+ g5 2.Qxg5+** *and*
3.Qxd8 *gains the Queen.*

#132 **1.Be5+ Kxe5 2.Qf4+** *and*
3.Qxc7. *The first skewer sets up
the second.*

#133 **1.Qb5+ Qxb5 2.e8/Q+** *and*
3.Qxb5

#134 **1.Qd6+ Kf5 2.Rxf7+ Ke4**
(**2...Kg4 3.Qxg6#**)
3.Qxc6+ *and takes on f3.*

#135 **1.Nd8 g5** (*else White's next move
is mate*) **2.h5 g4
3.Rf7+ Kg5 4.Rxf2**

#136 **1.Rh6+ Ke5 2.Re6+ Kf5
3.Rxe4** *wins the Knight.*

#137 **1.Rc8+ Rxc8 2.a8/Q Rxa8
3.Rxa8+ Ke7 4.Rxh8**

#138 **1...Qf4+ 2.Ke1 Qf1+
3.Kd2 Qe2+** *and* **4...Qxa2**

#139 **1.e6+ Kf8 2.Qxh8+ Bxh8
3.Rxh8+ Kg7 4.Rxe8**

#140 **1.Re2+ Kf1 2.Re1+ Kf2
3.R6e2+ Kf3 4.Re3+ Kg4
5.Rxh3** *gains the Queen.*

#141 **1.Re2+ Kf1 2.Re1+ Kf2
3.R7e2+ Kf3 4.Rf1+ Kxe2
5.Rxf8**

#142 **1.f6 Qxd7 2.Qxh7+ Ke6**
(**2...Ke8 3.Qg8#**) **3.Qxd7+
Kxd7 4.g4 Ke6 5.g5** *and the
endgame is an easy win.*

#143 1...Qh3 *and there's no way to save the d3-Bishop without losing the c3-Knight.*

#144 1.Rxd3 Qxd3 2.Rd1 Q-moves 3.Rxd8+

#145 1.Be3 Qxb2 2.Rb1 Q-moves 3.Bxc5

#146 1.Bg5 Rxd5 2.Bxe7 Ra5 3.Rd1 *wins.*

#147 1...Nxh2 2.Qxh5 Rxf1+ 3.Kxh2 gxh5 *and Black picks up either the c1-Bishop or the b1-Knight.*

#148 1.Nf6+ Kg7 2.Nxd7 Rxd7 3.Bxf5 *and Bishop takes Rook.*

#149 1.Ra1 (A) 1...Bc5 2.Bxc6 Nxc6 3.Rc1 *wins Bishop or Knight.* (B) 1...Bxd7 2.Rxa7 *and* 3.Rxd7

#150 1.Nf3 Qxd1 2.Rxd1 Re6 3.e5 Bxe5 4.Nxe5 Rxe5 5.Rxd7

#151 1.Nb6+ axb6 2.Ra3#

#152 1...Qxf4+ 2.Kxf4 Bh6#

#153 1.Bg5+ Kg8 (or ...Kg7) 2.Qh7#

#154 1.Qxe6+ fxe6 (1...Be7 2.Qxe7#) 2.Bg6#

#155 1...Qf3+ 2.Kh4 Qg3# *Or* 2.Kh2 Qg2#

#156 1.Qxh7+ Nxh7 2.Nf7# *Or* 1.Nf7+ Nxf7 2.Qxh7#

#157 1.Kf4 g5+ 2.Kf3 *and* 3.Ng6#

#158 1...Qxf2+ 2.Rxf2 Re1+ 3.Rf1 Rxf1#

#159 1.Rg7+ Kf2 2.Rf7+ Kg1 3.Re1#

#160 1.Rd8+ Rxd8 2.Qf8+ Rxf8 3.Ne7#

#161 1...Qxb2+ 2.Rxb2 Re1+ 3.Qd1 Rxd1#

#162 1.Rxg7+ Kxg7 2.Qf7+ Kh8 3.Qh7#

#163 1.Ng6+ hxg6 2.Qh3+ Qh4 3.Qxh4#

#164 1.Rxg6+ Kh5 (1...fxg6 2.Qxg6#) 2.Qe5+ *and* 3.Qh8#

#165 1.Qxh7+ Ke6 2.Qg6+ Bxg6 3.Rf6#

#166 1.Rf5 (*threatening mainly* 2.Qxh6+ Kxh6 3.Rh5#) 1...exf5 2.Nxf5 *along with* 3.Qxh6(+) *and* 4.Qg7#

#167 1.Qg8+ Rxg8 2.Nxg6+ Kh7 3.Ne5+ Kh8 4.Nf7#

#168 1...Qh4+ 2.Kg1 Bh2+ 3.Kh1 Bg3+ 4.Kg1 Qh2#

#169 1.Qg6+ fxg6 2.Bg8+ Kh8 3.Bf7+ Kh7 4.Bxg6#

#170 1.Bxh7+ Rxh7 2.Rxh7 Kxh7 3.Qh8+ Kg6 4.Qh5#

#171 1.Nf7+ Kg8 2.Nh6+ Kh8 3.Qg8+ Rxg8 4.Nf7#

#172 **1.Qxf6+ Rg7 2.Qf8+ Qxf8
(2...Rg8 3.Be5#)
3.exf8/Q+ Rg8 4.Be5#**

#173 **1...Qe3+ 2.Kh1 Nf2+
3.Kg1 Nd1+ 4.Kh1
(4.Kf1 Qf2#) 4...Qe1#**

#174 **1.g4+ fxg4 2.Nxg4+
(A)2...Qxb5 3.Nf6#
(B)2...g5 3.Qe8+ Qg6
4.Nf6#
(C)2...Rc5 3.Nf6+ Qxf6
4.Qe2#**

#175 *There's no answer to* **1...Bf8!** *and*
2...Rg8 *followed by mate on g2
or h2 or even g1. White can drag
things out by* **2.Bd7 Kxd7 3.d4
Rg8
4.Bg5 Rxg5** *but it's mate next
move.*

#176 **1...Qh1+ 2.Ke2 Bc4+
3.Ke3 Qf3+ 4.Kd4 Qd3+
5.Ke5 Qd5#**

#177 **1...Qd6+ 2.g3 Qd2+
3.Be2 Qxe2+ 4.Qf2 Qxf2#**

#178 **1...Qa2!** *(threatens* **2...Qf7#)**
2.Qd7+ *(2.hxg5 Qh2#)* **2...
Qf7+ 3.Qxf7+ Kxf7** *and
Black wins the King and pawn
endgame. E.g.* **4.hxg5 c5 5.gxf6
c4 6.g5 c3 7.g6+ Kxf6
8.Kh6 c2 9.g7 c1/Q+**

#179 **1...Qe2
(A) 2.Rxe2 Rf1#
(B)2.Bxf2 Qxf2+
3.Kh1 Qxe1#
(C)2.Qc1 Rxg2+ 3.Kh2
Rxh2+ 4.Kg1 Qg2#**

#180 **1.Qh4+ Kg8 2.Qf6** *and there's
no valid defense against* **3.Rh4** *and*
4.Rh8#

#181 **1.Ne6** *(threatens* **2.Qxg7#)**
**(A)1...fxe6 2.Qxg7#
(B)1...Nh5 2.Nxd8 Nxg3
3.Re8#**

#182 **1...Rf2+ 2.Ke4 d5+ 3.Rxd5**
(else **3.Kd3 or 3.Kd4 Rd2#)**
3...cxd5+ *and wins.*

#183 **1.Qh7** *(threatens* **2.Qxf7#)**
**(A)1...Nxh7 2.Rxf7#
(B)1...Re7 2.Qh8+ Ng8
3.Qxg8#**
*Black can stop mate by coughing up
material, starting with* **1...Ne5.**

#184 **1...f3** *(threatens* **2...Rh1#)**
**(A)2.Qxf3 Rxf3
(B)2.exf3 Rh1+
3.Kg2 Qh3#
(C) 2.Ke1 Qxe2#**

#185 **1...Bxh3 2.Qh2 Rxg2
3.Qxd6 Rxa2** *and there's nothing to be done against the coming
Bishop discovery.*

#186 **1...Rd4+ 2.Kg5** *(2.Kxh5
Rxf5#)* **2...Nf6!** *(threatens* **3...
h6#)** **3.f4 Ne4+** *forking King
and Queen.*

#187 **1.Nxe7+ Rxe7 2.Bxf6 gxf6
3.Ra8+ Re8 4.Rxe8#**

#188 **1.Rh8+ Kg7 (1...Bxh8
2.Rxh8#) 2.f4** *and the Bishop is
lost. Black can't afford* **2...Bxc3
3.Qxc3+ f6 4.Qxf6#**

#189 **1.Qh4 f6 2.Rxf8+ Kg7
(or 2...Qxf8 3.Qxh7#)
3.Qxh7+ Kxf8 4.Qh8#**

#190 **1.Rd1** *wins the Queen. If* **1...
Qxc2 2.Qa8+ Ke7
3.Qxb7+ (or 3.Qd8+) 3...
Ke6 4.Qd7#**

#191 **1.Rxg6+ fxg6 2.Qxg6+ Bg7 3.Qxe6+** *wins. If* **3...Kh8 4.Rxh4+** *And if* **3...Kf8** *then* **4.Rf1+**

#192 *The main line runs* **1.Nb5 cxb5 2.Bxb5+ Bd7 3.Bxd7+ Kd8 4.Bc8+** *and* **5.Qd8#**

#193 **1.Rxh6+ gxh6 2.Qxh6+ Kg8 3.Qxg6+ Kh8 4.Bxf7 Rxf7** (*else* **5.Qh6#**) **5.Qxf7** *and White is three pawns up in the Queen ending.*

#194 **1...Qb6+ 2.Kh1 Qf6 3.Rxh7 Qf1+ 4 Qg1 Qf3+ 5.Qg2 Qxg2#**

#195 **1...Nxh3+ 2.Kg2 Nf4+ 3.Kg1 Ne2+ 4.Qxe2 Qh2+ 5.Kf1 Qh1#**

#196 **1.Qb3+ Ka5** (**1...Kc7 2.Rxc6+** *and* **3.Qxf7**) **2.Rxc6 Qxb3** (**2...Qe7 3.Qc3+** *and mates next move*) **3.axb3+ Kb5 4.Nd4+ Kb4 5.Rc4#**

#197 **1...Ne3+ 2.Kg1** (**2.fxg3 Qc2+** *and* **3...Qxd1** *wins*) **2... Qc2 3.Rf1 Rxd3!** *wins since* **4.Qd7** *can be answered by* **4... Qxf2+ 5.Rxf2 Rd1+ 6.Rf1 Rxf1#**

#198 **1.Nxe5** (**A**)**1...Nxe5 2.Rxf8+ Kxf8 3.Qf4+ Nf7 4.Rf1** *wins.* (**B**) **1...Rxf1+ 2.Rxf1 Nxe5 3.Qf4 Ng6 4.Qf7+ Kh8 5.Qf8+ Nxf8 6.Rxf8#**

#199 **1.Nxf7 Rxf7 2.Rxf7 Kxf7 3.Qh7+ Kf8 4.Qh8+ Kf7 5.Qe8+ Kg7 6.Re7+ Kh6**

#200 **7.Re6** *winning Black's Queen, since* **8.Qxg6#** *is also threatened.*

#200 **1...Nxh2+ 2.Ke1 Nf3+ 3.Kf1 Rd1+ 4.Kg2 Rg1+ 5.Kh3 Rh1+ 6.Kg2** (**if 6.Kg4 h5#**) **6...Rh2+ 7.Kf1 Nd2+ 8.Ke1 Rh1#** *White can avoid mate only by giving up his Rook for Black's Knight at some stage.*

#201 **1.Nd5!** *The Knight can't be taken,* **1...Nxd5 2.Rxe8+** *And meanwhile, there's no defense against* **2.Nxf6+** *and* **3.Rxe8.**

#202 **1.Rxd7 Qxd7** (**1...Nxd7?? 2.Bxe7**) **2.Bxf6 Bxf6 3.Qxf6** *wins two pieces for the Rook, leaving White a pawn ahead in the end-game.*

#203 **1...Rxf1+** (**A**) **2.Kxf1 Qf2#** (**B**) **2.Rxf1 Qxh2#**

#204 **1.Ne4** *wins the d-pawn after* **1... Qxe4 2.Qxe4 Nxe4 3.Bxd5** *Or* **1...Qd6 2.Nxf6+ Rxf6 3.Qxd5+**

#205 **1.Rxe6 Rxe6 2.Qf7+** *and* **3.Qxg8**

#206 **1...Qb6+ 2.Qxb6 Bxb6+** *and* **3...Rxd7** *leaves Black the exchange ahead.*

#207 **1.Nxb4 axb4 2.Bxd5+** *and* **3.Bxa8**

#208 **1.Bxd7 Kxd7 2.Qb7+** *picks up the Bishop with more to come.*

#209 **1.Rxe7 Qxe7 2.Qg6+ Kh8 3.Qxh6#** *or* **3.Qxg7#**

#210 1.Rxe6 fxe6 2.Qxg7 Rf8
(2...Bf6 3.Nd6#) 3.Nc7+
wins the Black Queen.

#211 1.f6 Qxf6 (1...Rxh1+
2.Qxh1 *check!*)
2.Qxf6+ Nxf6 3.Rxh4+

#212 1.Bxc6 bxc6 2.Rxh7+ Qxh7
3.Qxf6+ *and* 4.Qxd8+ *gaining
a full piece.*

#213 1...Rxc6 2.Rxc6 Rxg2+
3.Kh3 Kf3 *and* 4...Rf2#

#214 1.Nxe5 Nxe5 2.Qxd6 cxd6
3.Be7 *wins the exchange.*

#215 1...Rxc3 2.Qxc3 Bb5+
3.Ke1 (3.Kg1 Qh2#) 3...
Bb4 *pins and wins the Queen.*

#216 1.Nxd7 Qxd7 (1...Qxc4
2.Rb8+ Bf8 3.Rxf8#)
2.Ne4 Rd5 3.Nxd6 *and Black
has no time to recapture the Knight
in view of*
4.Rb8+. *Essentially a Removing
the Guard tactic (the Nd7 and Bd6)
with an unpin and corridor mate
thrown in.*

#217 1...Bxb3 2.Nxb3 Nd4+
3.Nxd4 cxd4 4.Bxb4
(4.Bc7 b3 *and the pawn
promotes*) 4...Bxb4

#218 1...Nxd2+ 2.Bxd2 Qxe2
3.Bxe2 Rxe2 4.Rxe2 Bxd3+
and 5...Bxe2.

#219 1.Rxc8 Rxc8 2.Rd8+ Re8
3.Rxe8+ Rxe8 4.Nd5 Kf7
(4...Rc8 5.Ne7+) 5.Nb6 *and*
6.c8/Q *wins the Rook.*

#220 1.Rxc8+ Kxc8 (1...Rxc8
2.Ne6#) 2.Rc7+ Kb8 (2...
Kd8 3.Ne6+ *and*
4.Re7#) 3.Rxb7+ Kc8
4.Ne6 (*threatening among other
things* 5.d7+ Nxd7
6.Rc7+ Kb8 7.Rxd7)
(A)4...Ne4 5.Bxe4 fxe4
6.Rc7+ Kb8 7.Nxd4
and 8.Nc6+ *is decisive*
(B)4...Re8 5.Rc7+ Kb8
6.Nxd4 Re1+ 7.Bf1 *and
again* 8.Nc6+ *is coming up.
Another, totally different approach
is* 1.Bxb7 gxf4 (1...Bxb7
2.Ne6#) 2.Bxa8 *winning
the exchange. If* 1...Rb8, *then*
2.Rxc8+ *and* 3.Ne6#

#221 1.Bxa6
(A) 1...Qxa6 2.Qxc5
(B) 1...Nxa6 2.Qxb6

#222 1...Rxc2 2.Qxc2 Qxh4+ *and*
3...Qxe1 *Black can also start
with* 1...Qxh4+

#223 1...Rxd1+ 2.Rxd1 Qxc3
or Black may begin with 1...Qxc3
2.Rxc3 Rxd1+
3.Qf1 Rxf1+ *The second method
is preferable since it also gets the
Queens off the board, making it
harder for White to stage a come-
back.*

#224 1...fxe4 2.Qxe4 Nxe2+ *and*
3...Bxd5. *If the Queen drops
back,* 2.Qd1, *the d5-Knight falls
anyway.*

#225 1.Qf6 Qxd4 2.Qxd4 Rxd4
3.Re8#

#226 1.Bxc7 Qxc7 2.Rxe6 fxe6
3.Qxg6+

#227 **1.Rxf5 gxf5 2.Qh8+ Kf7 3.Bh5#** *An overload as the g6-Pawn cannot guard both f5 and h5.*

#228 **1.Nxg6+ fxg6 2.Rxe6** *with further gains to come. E.g.* **2... Kf7? 3.Rxf6+ Kxf6 4.Be5+** *and* **5.Bxh8**

#229 **1.Bxc7 Nxe4** (**1...Rxc7 2.Rxd6**) **2.fxe4** *wins a pawn. For if* **2...Rxc7 3.Rd8+ Qe8 4.Rxe8#**

#230 **1.Be7 Re8 2.Bxc5** *gains a full Knight:* **2...Rxe3 3.Bxe3 or 2...Qxc5 3.Rxe8+** *So after* **1.Be7** *Black has to let White win the exchange.*

#231 **1...Rd1+** (**A**) **2.Rxd1 Nxb4** (**B**) **2.Kxd1 Nxc3+** *and wins the Queen. A combination of deflection and attraction.*

#232 **1.Bd6** (*threatens* **2.Bxf8 Rxf8 3.Qg7#**) *and if* **1...Bxd6?? 2.Qg7** *mates immediately. The best Black can do is trade Queens by* **1...Qxh3 2.Bxf8 Qg4+** *but that leaves him a piece behind.*

#233 *Black's Queen is indirectly defended:* **1.Rxe2? Ba3+ 2.Kb1 Rd1#** *But* **1.Qxf8+!** *upsets Black's apple cart:* **1...Rxf8 2.Rxe2** *winning a piece.*

#234 **1.Rc8+ Rxc8 2.Rxc8+** *and* **3.Qxd4**

#235 **1.Bf4! Qg7 2.Be5** *and* **3.Qxh7#** *There is no way for the Black Queen to guard both e5 and h7.*

#236 **1...Bb5! 2.Qxb5** (**2.Rxb5 Rxc4**) **2...Qxe4+** *and* **3... Qxh1**

#237 **1.Nf7+ Rxf7 2.Bxf7 Qxf7** (**2...Nxf7 3.Qxh7#**) **3.Qd8+ Ne8 4.Qxe8+ Qxe8 5.Nxe8** *and White is up a pawn and the exchange.*

#238 **1.Qe5 Rd8** (**1...Ke7 2.Qg7+ Kd8 3.Qf8+**) **2.Rd7+! Rxd7** (*else Black gets mated*) **3.Qxb8** *wins the Queen.*

#239 **1...e3+ 2.Kxe3 Rxe1** *wins a piece. White has no time for* **3.Kxd4 Rd1+** *followed by Queening the e2-pawn.*

#240 **1...Bc4 2.Qxc4 Qd1+ 3.Qf1 Bxf2+ 4.Kh1 Qxf1#** *If* **2.Qxd8 Rxd8** *threatens* **3... Rxa8** *and mostly* **3...Rd1#**

#241 **1...Be6 2.Nd5** (**2.Qa3 Nc2 3.Qa5 Nxe3+** *and* **4...Nxd1**) **2...Nxe4** *and the pinned d5-Knight falls.*

#242 **1.Re7+ Rxe7 2.Rxe7 Kh6 3.Qxf6** *and White comes away with a full Queen.*

#243 **1.Ne2 Rxe4 2.Qf5+ Kh8 3.Rg8#**

#244 **1.Bxe5 Bxe5 2.b4 Rc4 3.Nxe5** *Better to give the exchange right away with* **1...Rxe5,** *which should lose in the long run.*

#245 **1.Nxe6 Nxg4 2.Ne7+ Kh8 3.Nxf8** *wins a full Rook.*

#246 **1.Nc6 Rd5 2.e4 fxe4 3.fxe4** *and Black has to yield the exchange by* **3...Rxd1.** *If* **1... Rc8** *then* **2.Nxe7 Kxe7 3.b4** *wins the pinned Knight.*

#247 **1...Nc6 2.Qb6 Qa3+ 3.Rb3 Qc1+ 4.Kd3 Bxc4#**

#248 **1...g6 2.Nxf6 Nf5+ 3.Kh2** (*or* **3.exf5 Qxh3#**) **3...Nxe3 4.Nxh7 Nxd1**

#249 **1.Nc7+ Kd7 2.Qxg5 Bxg5 3.Rxf8 Kxc7 4.Rxf7+ Bd7 5.Rxg7** *simplifying and picking up two pawns in the process.*

#250 **1...Rxf7 2.Bxf7 Ne5** *pushing the Rook off the 3rd rank. E.g.* **3.Rc3 Rxc3 4.bxc3 Nxf7 5.Qxf7 Qxg3.** *If* **3.Rd5** *then* **3...Rc1+ 4.Kh2** (*both* **4.Kf2** *and* **4.Nf1** *are met by* **4...Qf4**) **4...Ng4+ 5.hxg4 Qh4#** *Relatively best for White is to concede the exchange with 3.Bd5 Nxd3.*

#251 **1.Qb4** *combines two threats:* **2.Qxb4 and 2.Qb8+** *with a back row mate. Black cannot stop both.*

#252 **1.Re6** *threatens Queen mate at c7 along with the win of the Black Queen.*

#253 **1.Qh1** *threatens* **2.Qxh7#** *and* **2.Qxa1.**

#254 **1...Be4 2.Rxd6 Rh1#** *Or* **2.Bc1 Bxd5** *winning the Rook.*

#255 **1...Qg3** *threatens* **2...Qxg6,** *also* **2...Qxf2+ 3.Kh1 Qxd2**

#256 **1...Nh5** *stops the mate threat at g7. After* **2.Bxh5 Qxh6** *two White pieces are still under fire: Nd4 and Bh5.*

#257 **1...Qd3!** *is a triple threat:* **2... Qf1#;** **2...Kxe8;** *and* **2... Qxf3+** *It's much better than* **1... Kxe8?** *running into* **2.Nf6+** *and* **3.Bxd5.** *If White now responds with* **2.Be2,** *then* **2...Qb1+ and 3....Kxe8.** *But not the over-hasty* **2...Qxe2? 3.Nd6+** *and* **4.Rxe2.**

#258 **1.Rd2 Rxd2 2.Bxd2 Q-moves 3.fxg7** *wins a Bishop.*

#259 **1...Qb6 2.0-0-0 Qxf6** *winning two pieces for a Rook. If* **2.Rxg7+ Bxg7** *also wins two pieces for the Rook as there is no time to take the Bishop:* **3.fxg7? Qg1#**

#260 **1.Qf3 Rb8 2.Rd1 Nd7 3.Qxf8+ Nxf8 4.Rxd4+** *wins the exchange.*

#261 **1.Bd7** (*not* **1.Rxh4? Qg5+**) **1...Rd8 2.Rxh4 Rxd7** (**2... Qg5+ 3.Rg4**) **3.Qxh7+ Kf8 4.Rxd7 wins.** *E.g:* **4...Qg5+ 5.Kh1 Qc1+ 6.Kg2 Qc6+ 7.Qe4 Qxd7 8.Rh8#**

#262 **1.Qf3** (*threatens* **2.Rxd7** *as well as* **2.Qxh5**) **1...Rfd8 2.Qxh5 Qxc3** (**2...Be6** *also loses to* **3.Qxh7+ Kf8 4.Qh8+ Ke7 5.Rc7+** *etc.*) **3.Qxf7+ Kh8 4.Qh5+ Kg8 5.Qh7+ Kf8 6.Qh8+ Ke7 7.Qxg7+ Ke8 8.Qf7#**

#263 **1...Nc5 2.Qa7 Ra8** *snags the Queen.*

#264 **1.Bg5 Qd4 2.Ne2** *snares the Queen right in the middle of the board.*

#265 **1.g4 Qc2 2.Rd2** *and there is no escape.*

#266 **1.b4** *catches the Queen. If* **1... Qc8** *(or* **...Qc6**) *then* **2.Ne7+** *forks King and Queen.*

#267 **1...d4 2.cxd4 cxd4** *and the e3-Bishop has nowhere to run.*

#268 **1.Qg6** *and the Black Rook has no safe square.* **1...Rh7** *self-blocks and allows* **2.Qe8+ Bf8 3.Qxf8#**

#269 *After* **1.Qc5** *the Rook has no escape:* **1...Rxb7 2.Qc6+ Ke7 3.Qxb7** *and the passed b-pawn will cost Black another Rook.*

#270 **1.Ra4** *leaves the Knight no way out.* **(A)1...Nxa5 2.Qxa6 bxa6 3.Rxa5 (B)1...b5 2.axb6 (C)1...Nxe5 2.Qxa6** *and* **3.dxe5**

#271 **1...Ne4+ 2.Kg2 f5 3.Qe1 Bb4** *checkmates the Queen.*

#272 **1.Nd5 Qa4** *(no better are* **1... Nxa1** *or* **1...Qxf2+) 2.axb3 Qxb3 3.Ra3** *winning the Queen for Rook and minor piece.*

#273 **1.Ra4!** *threatens to trap the Queen by* **2.Bc1.** *The best way out for Black is likely* **1...a6 2.Bc1 axb5 3.Rxa8** *but after* **3...Qc3** *(not* **3...Qb4? 4.Ba3) 4.Bxb5** *White is up material.*

#274 **1...b4 (A) 2.Bd4 g4 (B) 2.Bd2 g4 3.Bh6 Rh8** *and Black wins a piece.*

#275 **1.g4 hxg4** *(else* **2.gxh5) 2.h5** *and the pawn runs in for a Queen.*

#276 **1...Rxh5+ 2.Rxh5 Rh6** *wipes off the Rooks, after which the a-pawn is unstoppable.*

#277 **1...Nxb5** *and if* **2.axb5 a4 wins.** *White can't stop both the a-pawn and the f-pawn.*

#278 **1.Qxe6+ Qxe6 2.d7 Qxd7** *(else White makes a new Queen)* **3.Rxd7** *and White has an extra Rook.*

#279 **1.Bxg6 hxg6 2.Bxd8 Kxd8 3.h7** *and* **4.h8/Q(+)**

#280 **1...Re3+ 2.Kxe3 (2.Kf4 Ra3) 2...Bc5+ 3.Kd3 Bxa7** *and promotes next move.*

#281 **1...Qa6+ 2.c4** *(or* **2.K-moves) 2...Qxa2 3.Rxa2 bxa2** *and makes a new Queen.*

#282 **1...Rd8** *(threatens* **2...Rxd2 3.Kxd2 f1/Q) 2.Rd3 (if 2.Nf1 Rd1+) 2...Rxd3 3.cxd3 Be2** *and the f-pawn costs White his Knight.*

#283   **1.e7+ Kxd7 2.Kf7 Bc4+ 3.Kf8** *and* **4.e8/Q(+)**

#284   **1.Rxd2 Qb4** (**1...Qxd2? 2.Qxf8#**) **2.Qxf8+ Qxf8 3.Rc2** *followed by* **4.Rc8** *and promotion of the b-pawn.*

#285   **1.c6+ Kb6 2.Rxa6+ Nxa6 3.Rxa6+ Kxa6 4.c7** *and promotes next move.*

#286   **1...Kxc4!** (*not* **1...cxd4? 2 c5,** *nor* **1...exd4? 2.e5** *and White wins*) **2.dxe5** (**or 2.d5 Kb5!** *which also wins for Black*) **2...Kb5 3.e6 Kc6 4.e5 g5.** *The White pawns are stopped and one of Black's pawns gets through to Queen.*

#287   **1.Qf2 Qxf2 2.Ra8+ Kxa8** *stalemate.*

#288   **1...Qxc4 2.dxc4 a5** *and White is unable to release the stalemate on Black's King.*

#289   **1.h8/Q+ Ke4 2.Qh1+! Qxh1** *stalemate.*

#290   **1...Bc6+! 2.Qxc6 Rg1+ 3.Kxg1** *stalemate.*

#291   *White threatens* **1.Rbg8** *and* **2.Rh4#** *So Black scurries for the draw by* **1...Rxf2+! 2.Kxf2 Qxe3+ 3.Kxe3** *stalemate.*

#292   *The King takes shelter in the corner:* **1.Ka1 Kxc3** *stalemate. Or* **1...Kc2 2.Be5 c3 3.Bxc3 Kxc3** *and it's still stalemate. Another try after* **1.Ka1** *is* **1...Bd1 2.Be5 c3 3.Bxc3 Kxc3 4.Kxa2** *but*

Black can't win with his remaining Rook's pawn since his Bishop doesn't control the Queening square a1.

#293   **1.h3 Nd6 2.Rh7+ Kg8 3.Rg7+ Kf8 4.Rf7+ Ke8 5.Re7+ Kd8 6.Rd7+** *and now Black must take the Rook,* **6... Kxd7** *stalemate. He can't afford* **6...Kc8 7.Rxd6** *with* **Rxg6** *to follow.*

#294   **1.Qxe4+ Kxe4 2.f3+ gxf3 3.Kf2 Ke5 4.Kxf3** *and it's a book draw. This is the stuff you've got to know.*

#295   **1.Ne5 Rd6 2.Nf7+ Kg6 3.Ne5+** (*don't take the Rook, take the draw*) **3...Kh6 4.Nf7+** *etc. White keeps checking endlessly.*

#296   **1.Nd7 Bxd7** (**1...Qb5 2.Nxe5 Rxe5 3.Qf6** *favors White*) **2.Qf7+ Kh8 3.Qf8+ Kh7 4.Qf7+** *with perpetual check.*

#297   **1.Rxh7! Bxe3** (**1...Rxf6** *and* **1...Kxh7** *both lose to* **2.Qh3+**) **2.Rh8+ Kf7 3.Rh7+** c*heck, check, check.*

#298   **1...Qxf1+ 2.Kxf1 Rd1+ 3.Kf2** (**3.Be1 Rdxe1+ 4.Kf2 Bh4+! 5.g3 R4e2#**) **3...Rd2+ 4.Kf1 Rd1+** *etc.*

#299   **1.Qe8+ Kh7 2.Ng5+ hxg5 3.Qh5+ Kg8 4.Qe8+** *etc.*

#300   **1...Qc5+ 2.Kh1** (**2.Kg2? Qf2+**) **2...Ng3+ 3.hxg3 Qc1+ 4.Kg2 Qd2+ 5.Kh3 Qh6+** *with continuous checks from c1, d2, and h6.*

#301 **1...Ra2+ 2.Kh3 Rh2+
3.Kxh2 Ra2+ 4.Kh3 Rh2+
5.Kxh2 Qb2+ 6.Kh3 Qg2+
7.Kxg2** *stalemate.*

#302 **1.Be5 Rh4 2.Bg3 Rd4
3.Bf2 Rxd7 4.Kc3! Kc5
5.Be3** and *Black cannot make
progress. Another thing you should
know: normally King + Rook vs.
King + Bishop is a draw.*

#303 **1.Rxe7! Qxh4+ 2.Kg1 Qxg5
3.Rxa7+ Kb4 4.Rb7!** *Winning Black's last Pawn. Since White
now has slight winning chances,
Black should bail out with* **4...
Qe3+**, *which leads to perpetual
check. This is the type of practical
decision (forcing a slightly favorable
simplification from a dangerous, un-
clear position) which you must learn
to make in order to play good chess.*

LOTTERY SUPER SYSTEM
LotterySuperSystem.com

WIN MONEY PLAYING THE LOTTERY—FINALLY!

Lottery Super System is jam packed with super-charged strategies specifically designed to beat the lotto and lottery. Based on Prof. Jones Gold and Platinum lotto and lottery systems, and now fully upgraded, expanded and modernized for today's games, Lottery Super System is the result of thirty years of intense scientific research and testing, and the result is the most powerful arsenal of winning programs ever developed.

FIVE POWER STRATEGIES ARE INCLUDED!

The heart of Lottery Super System is its five power strategies—a formidable 100-game regression analysis (plus models with even stronger engines), best number analysis, overdue analysis, cluster analysis, and lucky number analysis. Also included in the Lottery Super System engine are full computer-generated wheeling systems to optimize all your bets into the specified number of lotto and lottery tickets you choose. We also include an instructional guide on how to use our wheeling systems to win millions and millions of dollars. Lottery Super System contains individual modules optimized for all 3 ball, 4 ball, 5 ball, and 6 ball lotto and lottery games from 6/35 to 6/54, multistate games such as Powerball and Mega Millions, and every major lottery and lotto game.

EXOTIC SYSTEMS & FREE WINNING DRAWS!

Lottery Super System features all the bells, whistles and goodies you expect from a premier power program, *and* includes exotic wagering systems for bettors who don't follow the pack. You also get FREE access to every lotto and lottery drawing in all states so you can go back and track winning balls and combinations to use in all your strategies. What balls are hot? What balls are not? It's alvailable FREE on Lottery Syper System.

WIN $10,000,000 OR MORE PLAYING THE LOTTERY!!!

Imagine if you win $10,000,000 with the Lottery Super Systems! It could happen, and it could happen to you! Maybe you'll win less, maybe even more. But one thing we can promise you: Your chances of winning small jackpots and big million-dollar jackpots will immediately double, triple, and even increase tenfold!

Sound too good to be true? Go to our website now to get all your questions answered and to see all the features of this winning program and how it can instantly increase your chances of winning results!

Go Online Now!
LotterySuperSystem.com

192